Varieties of Relativism

In memory of Bimal Matilal,
colleague and friend.

Varieties of Relativism

*Rom Harré &
Michael Krausz*

BLACKWELL
Oxford UK & Cambridge USA

First published 1996

2 4 6 8 10 9 7 5 3 1

Blackwell Publishers Ltd
108 Cowley Road
Oxford OX4 1JF
UK

Blackwell Publishers Inc.
238 Main Street
Cambridge, Massachusetts 02142
USA

British Library Cataloguing in Publication Data

A CIP catalogue record for this book is available from the British Library.

Library of Congress Cataloging-in-Publication Data

Harré, Rom.
    Varieties of relativism / by Rom Harré and Michael Krausz.
        p. cm.
    Includes bibliographical references and index.
    ISBN 0–631–18409–0 (hardbound : alk. paper). — ISBN 0–631–18411–2 (pbk. : alk. paper)
    1. Relativism. I. Krausz, Michael. II. Title.
BD221.H36 1996
149—dc20   95–12473
                                                            CIP

Typeset in 11½ on 13½ pt Bembo by Photoprint, Torquay, Devon
Printed in Great Britain by Hartnolls Ltd, Bodmin, Cornwall

This book is printed on acid-free paper

Contents

Preface   vii

1 **The Debate**   1

   Introduction   1
   The Roots of Relativism   2
   Our Conceptual Tools   4
   The Arguments for Discursive Relativism
     in General   7
   Contemporary Relativism in Context   11
   The Basic Insights Spelled Out   16
   Varieties of Relativism   23
   The Shape of Anti-relativist Arguments   26
   Our Argumentative Strategy   32

2 **Semantic Relativism**   34

   Introduction   34
   Absolutist Accounts of Meaning   37
   The Argument for a Universal Root Vocabulary   41
   The Upshot of These Arguments   52
   Arguments for Semantic Relativism   53
   Conclusion   64

3 **Epistemic Relativism**   68

   Introduction   68
   Epistemic Frameworks   75
   A Global Argument Against Epistemic Relativism   94
   The Paradoxes of Epistemic Relativism   96

The Strong Programme: Is it a Sociological
  Reduction?   99
Some Standard Objections to the Strong
  Programme   104
The Strong Programme Reconsidered   107
Afterword   109

4 Ontological Relativism   **111**
Introduction   111
Some Arguments for Ontological Relativism   114
Possible Resolutions   125
Ontological Relativism and its Epistemic
  Groundings   135
A Paradox of Ontological Relativism   139
The Existence of Artifacts   141

5 Moral Relativism   **149**
Introduction   149
How we Might Distinguish Moralities from
  Practical Maxims   150
Some Arguments for Moral Relativism   156
Some Arguments for Moral Absolutism   165

6 From Relativism to Anarchy   **189**
Introduction   189
The Extremists: From Relativism to Anarchy   190

7 Residues and Resolutions   **207**
Introduction   207
Antinomies   209
Paradoxes   220
Our Position   222

References   **225**

Name Index   **232**

Subject Index   **234**

Preface

The advent of relativism, in the early 1970s, as a serious contender for the crown of philosophical orthodoxy in our time, has been followed by a vast proliferation of academic writings. Developments in fields other than philosophy have been recruited by advocates of relativism and by their opponents. The fact that the debate has continued for twenty years without resolution suggests that perhaps there are no conclusive arguments for relativism or absolutism. But it also suggests something else – that neither position is simple or univocal. In this study we have tried to bring out clearly some of the component doctrines that coalesce into absolutism, and by contrast to bring out the corresponding relativisms. Absolutists might be arguing for universalism, or objectivism or foundationalism, Relativists may be arguing against, one, two or all three of these species of absolutism. The result is a proliferation of varieties of relativism. By using this insight to clarify the arguments in each of the main fields of the relativist/absolutist debate – semantic, epistemic, ontological and moral relativism – we have tried to present the whole field as a complex pattern of inconclusive controversies. One can find good reasons for a relativist stance in the sense of denying that there are semantic universals while holding that the way the world is makes a difference to what we are entitled to believe, that is that there is a sense in which we can have objective knowledge. One can make sense of the debates of the last two decades only, we believe, by paying attention to the question of which of the species of absolutism this or that variety of relativism opposes.

In our efforts to present a clear and comprehensive account of the arguments for and against all sorts of varieties of relativism we have been greatly helped by friends and colleagues, whose critical commentaries on earlier drafts have been invaluable. We should mention particularly Joseph Margolis, Bernard Harrison, David Norton and Daniel Robinson.

We are grateful to the Editor of *Language Sciences* for permission to reproduce some passages from Volume 15, Number 3.

Rom Harré,
Linacre College, Oxford and Georgetown University,
Washington, D.C.

Michael Krausz,
Bryn Mawr College, Bryn Mawr, Pennsylvania.

1

The Debate

Introduction

The debate between relativists and absolutists is of great antiquity and seeming intractability. The literature on the subject is huge. The turns and twists of the argument are labyrinthine. What conceivable reason could there be for yet another book on the subject? Rather than adding to the pleas and counterpleas of the advocates of this or that form of relativism in this or that context or with respect to this or that subject matter, our aim is to extricate and examine the arguments, abstracted from sources ancient and modern, that have been offered for and against the main varieties of relativism. We have tried to take the simplest forms of the arguments for and against relativism and in support or subversion of absolutism. They have been arranged with respect to the major divisions of subject matters to which they have been applied: meaning, knowledge, existence and value. We have tried to bring out similarities and differences in the arguments. This is not an exegetical work. We are aiming at a presentation that would serve in the classroom to introduce the kinds of arguments that appear in particular texts. Authors have been mentioned in appropriate places, but this is not a critical exposition of the literature. As a general term for anti-relativisms of all varieties we have chosen the term 'absolutism', and we would like it to be read always in this generic sense, as referring to any view which is anti-relativist. Just as we hope to show that there are a variety of relativisms, so there are varieties of absolutisms, some idealist, some realist.

The Roots of Relativism

We might think that we could move freely from one context, epoch, culture, language or personal point of view to another taking our beliefs, customs and moral principles with us, unchanged. We might think that we could bring them to bear upon the beliefs, customs and moral principles of the inhabitants of other cultural and linguistic milieux. Furthermore we tend to think that we could, with a bit of an effort, come to understand the beliefs of others without ambiguity, that we could adopt the customs of other cultures and live their lives to the full, that we could assess the valuational criteria of other moral orders in comparison to our own. But the possibility of such cross-cultural transplantings and excursions makes sense only if certain fundamental conditions on the means of communication between the inhabitants of different cultures and epochs could be met. There would have to be a means of establishing a sufficiently reliable translatability between languages, or, what amounts to the same thing, one universal language into which the statements couched in any language and made by anyone in any possible circumstances could be translated without drastic loss of sense. There would have to be a common human nature upon which all possible legal and moral systems could be based and to which all possible aesthetic judgements could be referred. If these conditions could be met all accounts of how the world is, from whatever vantage point and animated by whatever theory, could finally be reconciled into one coherent story, a universal natural science. In the end we tend to think that all reasonable people would agree on meanings, morality and science. It is in the arguments that have tended to show that some or all of the conditions for this desirable unanimity *cannot* be met that Relativism is born.

Relativisms come in two broad flavours – the sceptical and the permissive. One demonstration seeks to prove that there is an indefinite number of points of view from which the world presents an irreducibly different appearance, that there is an indefinite number of mutually incompatible descriptions of and theories about its appearance, and that there are radically disjoint and irreconcilable judgements of the value of human conduct and human artifacts. These assertions have been used to support two broad theses:

1 *Scepticism*: no point of view is privileged, no description is true, and no assessment of value is valid.
2 *Permissiveness*: all points of view are equally privileged, all descriptions are true and all assessments of value are equally valid.

We could call these positions 'malign relativism' and 'benign relativism' respectively. This analysis is coarse-grained, and the variety of relativisms it reveals sharply polarized. Both Scepticism and Permissiveness stand in opposition to just one absolutism, which, if it could be established, would defeat them both. There would be one point of view from which the final truth of things could be unequivocally ascertained. Weaker forms of relativism are easily devised, by softening the demands of scientific and moral absolutism. Instead of requiring the inexorable pursuit of the ultimate truth about the world we might settle for the establishment of justified belief and yet contend that though there will be many systems of belief some are better supported than others. Instead of proselytizing for a universal set of moral principles we might settle for a common respect for persons licensing a variety of morally adequate systems for the evaluation of persons and their conduct. Instead of a reduction of appearances to the view from one and only vantage point we might admit the complementarity of many points of view.

Our Conceptual Tools

We have already introduced a terminology for the broad contrast between *absolutisms* and *relativisms*. In some cases we shall characterize relativisms directly, in others by contrast with whatever absolutism, in context, a species of relativism seems to repudiate or contradict.

A substantial part of our effort will be devoted to identifying which subspecies of absolutism is denied or contradicted by which variety of relativism. For this purpose we shall recognize three genera of absolutism, each appearing in a discursive and an ontological variant:

1   *universalism*:
    (a) discursive variant: there are beliefs (classes of statements) which hold good in all contexts, at all times and for all persons.
    (b) ontological variant: there are entities (classes of existents) which exist for all persons.

2 *objectivism*:
  (a) discursive variant: there are beliefs (classes of state-
      ments) which hold independently of the point of
      view, corpus of beliefs or conceptual scheme held
      to and employed by any particular person or
      society.
  (b) ontological variant: there are entities (classes of
      existents) which exist independently of the point of
      view, corpus of beliefs or conceptual scheme held to
      or employed by any particular person or society.
3 *foundationalism*:
  (a) discursive variant: there is a common set of basic
      statements, not capable of further analysis, which
      serve in each context for each kind of enquiry for
      the assessment of all judgements of a relevant kind.
  (b) ontological variant: there is a common ontology or
      set of basic existents, incapable of further analysis,
      out of which all other existents are constructed.

There are various patterns of opposition, contrast and
interconnection between the subspecies of these genera. In
the course of our detailed analyses of relativisms in their
home contexts, we shall be articulating some of these
patterns. Different patterns of contrast and interconnection will emerge as we identify the various species and
subspecies of these generic positions. It seems clear that in
some contexts universalism could be accepted while
objectivism and foundationalism were jointly or severally
rejected. We might believe that everyone would make the
same intuitive judgement of some famous artwork, without supposing that their common judgement was based on
some basic common protocol. It seems clear too that there
are some contexts in which if we accept objectivism we

must be committed to universalism, but not to foundationalism. For instance if we hold that there are some physical phenomena which are what they are independent of the people who come to know them, then we would expect every culture eventually to discover them, though in none would they play the role of foundations for knowledge. Finally there are contexts in which it seems that the acceptance of foundationalism requires that we must also accept objectivism and universalism. If we believe that all moral judgements rest finally on respect for persons we would also believe that this holds independently of tribal interests and for everyone.

At the outset it is worth emphasizing the logical independence of the three genera of absolutisms that we have identified. There are some varieties of relativism that are compatible with universalism, some with objectivism and some with foundationalism. Furthermore a belief can, in certain circumstances, be both objective and foundational without being held universally. For example, there were no doubt many objective and foundational beliefs held by the Etruscans which could never become universal since the key to their language seems to be irretrievably lost. A belief can be universal and objective and yet not foundational. For example everyone may believe rightly that water is the main constituent of the oceans and that this is so independently of whether anyone knows it or not, but such a belief does not serve as the foundation for *all* other beliefs in our culture, though it may support a good many. And a belief can be universal and foundational and not objective. For example there are certain phenomena which come into existence only in apparatus constructed by human beings. Beliefs about these phenomena may rightly be taken to be universal and foundational for the sciences, though, as artifacts, they could not be objective.

In the first five chapters of our study we shall be couching many of our arguments in terms of 'truth'. Considerations advanced in support of relativism or absolutism will be discussed with respect to concepts like 'belief', 'knowledge' and 'moral value'. But as Margolis (1993b) has pointed out, all such discussions presuppose a culture transcendent notion of 'truth' and its partner 'falsity'. Assessments of propositions as to their truth or falsity are called 'alethic' judgements. 'Alethic universality', that the 'true/false' distinction is universally and unambiguously applicable to all propositions, is presupposed in setting up 'epistemological relativism', the thesis that knowledge, that is *true* belief, is culture relative. In the final chapter we shall discuss the proposal that this tie too should be loosened and that we should consider too the possibility of alethic relativism, that the very concept of 'truth' is culture bound.

The Arguments for Discursive Relativism in General

All arguments for relativisms of whatever strength or variety depend on the observation that there are, as a matter of fact, many languages, many theories for every phenomenon, many descriptions of what can be felt, seen, touched and so on, and many differing assessments of moral and aesthetic values. From this observation it is concluded that phenomena are relative to which description is chosen, explanations are relative to which theory is favoured and both are relative to which language is used. By a parallel line of argument it is supposed that moral and aesthetic assessments are relative to whatever criteria are

current. To make this convincing we would need to argue
for the following theses:

1   Languages are never completely intertranslatable.
2   There are indefinitely many incompatible theories for
    each data base, meeting the same criteria of accept-
    ability.
3   There are indefinitely many incompatible systems of
    descriptive categories.
4   There are indefinitely many irreconcilable systems of
    moral and aesthetic values.

Arguments proliferate as the key notions such as inter-
translatability, incompatibility, irreducibility and so on are
spelled out in different ways.

  This general philosophical foundation for all discursive
relativisms can be condensed into four negative theses:

  I   There could be no universal language adequate to a
       common human world.
 II   There could be no unified theory universally appli-
       cable in all contexts at all times.
III   There could be no definitive system of descriptive
       categories picking out a common range of natural and
       social phenomena.
IV   There could be no universal moral/aesthetic princi-
       ples viable in all cultures at all times.

Only if the negative theses are expressed in the 'could be'
form, that is as necessary propositions, are they of philosophical interest. The four negative theses must, therefore,
be defended by relativists by philosophical argument,

rather than by inductions from empirical evidence. The fact that there are and have been thousands of languages in use in different times and places does not support Thesis I unless it can be shown that they could not be mutually translated. If there were perfect translatability between languages any one could serve as the universal tongue.

Important arguments have been offered for all four theses. The 'radical translation' argument of W.V. Quine (1975, 1969) has been proposed for Thesis I and will be discussed in chapter 2; the 'incommensurability of paradigms' argument of T.S. Kuhn (1970) has been used to support Thesis II, and will be discussed in chapter 3, and its ontological variant in chapter 4; the 'theory-ladenness of descriptions' argument, originated by Whewell (1847), has been used to defend Thesis III and will be discussed in chapter 4, while the 'independence of fact and value' argument, of Hume and others, has been given as a ground for Thesis IV and will be discussed in chapter 5. We shall show that none of these arguments is without problems. While we do not believe that there can be any final resolution of the debate between relativism in general and absolutism in general, nevertheless we do believe that various rapprochements are possible, context by context and case by case. It is to these that chapter 7 is devoted. However we shall also show that counterarguments purporting to establish corresponding and antithetical absolutisms have serious weaknesses too.

There is an important presupposition of all this, which will not have escaped the reader. The four general relativist theses have been presented in discursive forms. These forms each rest on ontological presuppositions, that there is something non-relative: namely, certain cultural and natural phenomena around which the many different and irreducible discourses cluster. Relativism takes its strongest form when the natural and social worlds and their phenomenal appearances are themselves claimed to be products of the language and other culturally distinctive practices of the persons who inhabit them. If there is no common world, natural or cultural, there could then be no privileged culture the members of which could, by relying on a common basis in experience, build a robust, unitary non-relativist account of the world, which could circumvent the differences between languages and other cultural practices.

We have formulated ontological relativism by talking of the natural and the social world together. Obviously the thesis that there is no common natural world which has been the common subject matter of the sciences since antiquity is a good deal stronger thesis than the denial that everyone inhabits a common social world. While we are inclined to deny the former claim we are sympathetic to at least some versions of the latter.

It is important to distinguish multiple world relativism from solipsism. Cultural and linguistic relativism tied to a doctrine of the relativity of worlds does not lead into a hopeless solipsism in which each human being occupies and is confined to a world of their own. In such a world there would be no languages, and the solipsistic lost soul would be unable even to frame this sceptical thought. Neither the idea of diverse languages nor of other cultures could have a part in the philosophical speculations of any one of these creatures. We shall not discuss this 'ultimate' version of relativism any further. For us the strongest form of relativism must be that in which a tribe, possessed of a public language and a common culture, considers and rejects the idea that it would be possible to enter into the worldly beliefs and the moral and aesthetic valuations of other tribes.

The theses of ontological relativism corresponding to the negative theses of discursive relativism can be expressed more briefly.

O1   There is no common world for all people.
O2   There is no universal system of real causal processes.
O3   There are no common natural or social phenomena for all people.
O4   There are no common human values.

Contemporary Relativism in Context

The concept of 'culture'

Relativism is often defined for a popular audience in the thesis that meaning, truth and value are relative to culture, that is each culture has its own unique systems of meaning, repertoire of truths and criteria of value. We shall be making use of the notion of 'culture' from time to time. But it is a concept that is ill-defined both as to its content and the boundaries of that to which it refers. As a working and conveniently vague characterization we shall take a culture to be an integrated system of symbolic and material practices, that is ways of achieving goals and projects that are constrained by local norms, and which are historical in that they emerge from and continue traditions.

The elements of culture in relation to diversity

Relativisms depend heavily on the thesis of the radical diversity of cultures: just what does that mean? There are various elements that go to make up a 'culture'. Each element, which might be alleged to vary from culture to culture, is tied in with certain aspects of everyday life. At this point discursive and ontological relativisms are inter-connected.

(1) *The 'psychological' element in culture*: There is an *internal relation* between the languages we speak and write and our psychologies (i.e. perceptual skills, our sense of self, the emotions we learn to display, the patterns of reasoning that we take to be compelling etc.). If we hold that languages are never perfectly translatable then we must accept that there will be likely to be some diversity in the psychological processes, states, phenomena etc. men-tioned above. For example it can be shown that the use of first person pronouns and of the first person inflexions of most languages differ in the degree to which they commit the speaker to the content and moral force of the utter-ances in which they occur. In communities of speakers of European languages using the first person commits the speaker as an individual, while for many oriental lan-guages such uses commit the group of which the speaker is at that moment and in that context taken to be a member. Japanese lacks a grammatical device for the expression of individual responsibility. The range of differences thereby revealed appears to be well correlated with different senses of 'selves'.

These and other observations provide the premises for a major argument for the cultural diversity of selfhood (Muhlhausler and Harré (1991)). Similar arguments have been offered by Lutz (1988) for a linguistically dis-tinguished variety in repertoires of emotions across cul-tures. Nature, it is supposed, provides every human being with a 'survival kit' of very generalized emotional re-actions, expressing highly non-specific judgements about what is dangerous, what is desirable and so on. The highly specific and complex systems of embodied judgements we call 'the emotions' are elaborations shaped by language, of the basic undifferentiated repertoire. By that it is meant that in learning one's language with the conditions for its proper use, one acquires the local emotion repertoire. The presumption in this case is that language drives culture.

(2) *The 'science' element in culture*: There is an *internal relation* between our beliefs and the phenomena we are able to observe, differentiate and identify. We use the term 'science' in this context because it is in relation to that enterprise that this point has come to the attention of philosophers in modern times. If we also believe that the theories that express the scientific element in a culture are never perfectly interrelatable, and that there are a diversity of scientific cultures, we must accept that there is a cultural diversity of phenomena. Since coherent clusters of scientific beliefs succeed each other in the history of science, this thesis entails that there is no scientific progress, only the substitution of one world picture with its associated 'facts' for another. There are no culturally independent facts of which we are getting a better and better grasp. For example one would have to say, if one believed Prout's hypothesis, that is the theory that the atoms of all elements are clusters of hydrogen atoms each of mass '1', one would expect that the atomic weights of all elements, relative to the atomic weight of hydrogen, would be whole numbers. Measurements which seemed to show that there were non-integral atomic weights, would have to be classed as errors. If all atoms are clusters of hydrogen atoms of mass 1, then the relative weights of all atoms must be multiples of 1. Berzelius' experimental confirmation of the discovery that atomic weights were not whole numbers, that is not integral multiples of the weight of a hydrogen atom, enforced by his immense 'moral authority', not only

served to change people's minds about the phenomena, that is which measurements were correct and which were errors, but it forced them to abandon the 'hydrogen' theory in which the idea that integral atomic weights were true phenomena was grounded. According to Whewell (1847) there is a cyclical and mutual interaction between experiment ('fact' gathering) and theory ('fact' interpreting). Accepting a certain theory makes certain 'facts' available. But these 'facts' are subjected to further experimental test, the results of which force refinements, which, in their turn, affect those beliefs we call theories. And so on.

(3)   *The 'social' element in culture*: The claim that there is an *internal relation* between belief-systems and social formations together with the thesis that belief-systems are never mutually subsumable entails radical diversity of social formations. For example what is held to be just, moral, legal etc. in some society is relative to the local belief-system, that is to the local conception of the nature of *homo sapiens*, of the role and meaning of the state, of civil society and so on.

Culture and the basic insights

The three basic insights on which contemporary relativism rests can be formulated in terms of the notion of a culture are as follows:

1   *The anthropological insight*: There are diverse cultures.
2   *The constructivist insight*: The main features of the world–as–experienced are determined by culture.
3   *The semantic insight*: The meanings of symbolic systems are functions of culture.

The discussion in the previous section of the way that aspects or elements of culture influence how we ourselves are, how our world appears to be and the way that we assess our conduct and the objects that our world appears to contain, implies that these three insights are interrelated in the context of relativism. Unless the anthropological insight were to be taken seriously neither the constructivist nor the semantic insights would recommend themselves. However if we ask what it means to claim that there are diverse cultures, it seems that it must mean that there are diverse ways of experiencing the world, and many diverse symbolic systems, among which is the diversity of languages on which so much emphasis has been placed.

These insights are not new. However in their earlier manifestations they were 'capped', that is seeming irresistible relativist conclusions were blocked by assumptions which were intrinsic to the positions of those who gave the most vigorous expression to these insights. We shall call these incipient but aborted relativisms, non-relativisms, distinguishing them from explicit absolutism or anti-relativisms.

Non-relativisms take two forms. We shall call them *extrinsic* and *intrinsic* non-relativisms. To clarify what we mean by this distinction we must distinguish between the *criteria of diversity* by which we recognize two alternative points of view, or two moral positions as diverse and different; and the *criteria of uniqueness* by which one of the diverse points of view or clashing moral systems is picked out as the right or the better or the more progressive one. In the case of extrinsic non-relativisms the criteria of diversity, the application of which enables us to identify a range of alternative points of view, say alternative basic moral positions, are differently grounded from the criteria of uniqueness by which one of these alternatives is picked out as the best. For example we might argue for moral relativism by citing diversity of conceptions of the worthwhile life as our way of demonstrating cultural diversity of moral positions, while offering a theological criterion, say Biblical revelation, as a way of selecting the uniquely best moral order. In the case of intrinsic nonrelativisms the criteria for demonstrating diversity, say of scientific paradigms, does not lead to relativism of belief because by the use of the very idea of scientific rationality a better or more advanced scientific paradigm can be picked out from the various paradigms on offer. We shall illustrate extrinsic non-relativism by a brief examination of Aristotle's primordial 'anthropological insight', that there are a diversity of political systems, and his non-relativist way of selecting the polis as the only proper system. We shall illustrate intrinsic non-relativism by a brief examination of the 'constructivist insight' as developed by Kant, in which the uniqueness of the twelve categories constrains the worlds we can synthesize. We shall say that these arguments are aimed at 'capping' or 'blocking' the surge towards relativism that comes from realizing that much of the structure of the world as we experience it is imported into that world by our perceptual and cognitive processes.

The Basic Insights Spelled Out

Aristotle: The anthropological insight

According to Aristotle there is a huge variety of actual political arrangements. A classification system can be devised based on six categories: monarchy, aristocracy, polity and tyranny, oligarchy and democracy. Permuting these gives a multiplicity of mixed forms, some of which can be found as the constitutions of real states. Does this lead to political relativism? No, because there is one and only one 'morally correct' state format, namely the polis, that formation in which the nature of Man can be fully realized. This type of formation can exist only in certain actual political arrangements. What distinguishes the polis from all other political formations? It is that political arrangement which sustains personhood among the citizens, and thus is defined as the best by moral rather than pragmatic criteria. The polis is to be admired because it offers its citizens the opportunity to cultivate virtue rather than merely securing the protection of the material goods of industrious citizens. This is an extrinsic blockage of the path to relativism, since the criteria for distinguishing one and only proper or best state formation are drawn from outside the domain of variety that creates the problem of incipient relativism.

In *Politics* Book III Chapter 9 Aristotle (1921) considers various criteria for demarcating a 'state', such as that which guarantees 'security from injustice', or commercial exchange. None are satisfactory. He concludes that 'a political society exists for the sake of noble actions, and not of mere companionship'. But what if there are many forms of government? If the virtue of the citizen and the virtue of the 'good man' are different 'the virtue of the citizen must be relative to the constitution of which he is a member.' It cannot be the case then that there is one single virtue of the good citizen 'which is perfect virtue.' Yet that must be true of the good man. The anthropological insight, the result of comparative studies, is this: '. . . in some states the good man and the good citizen are the same, and in others different.' Only those in which they are the same are exemplifications of the true polis. Why? Because in the polis, the perfect political arrangement, the state exists to bring virtuous men [and we would say 'people'] into being. Man's higher nature is characterized by the possession of reason, and this can be exercised only in the polis, through life under the rule of law, that is life managed in accordance with reason and referred, not to the whims of individual persons in authority, but to edicts, laws as propositions. The polis provides an ideal model or absolute standard of political value, related to the essence of humanity, namely reason.

The anthropological insight generalized

Aristotle's realization that there are many ways in which a state can be organized can be seen as a special case of the thesis of cultural diversity. That thesis runs something as follows: 'There are indefinitely many, relevantly distinct languages and associated sets of discursive and material practices, constituting relevantly distinct cultures.' There are two possible inferences to be drawn from this empir- ical observation. The weak relativist thesis: there is, as a matter of fact, no universal culture. This is still compatible with some way of ranking diverse forms of life, according to some absolute value. However there is also the strong relativist thesis: there could be no way of ranking actual cultures according to some absolute value. An additional premise would be needed to reach this terminus from the thesis of cultural diversity, and we shall later pursue the question of what that extra premise might be.

Kant: The constructivist insight

The world as we know it and ourselves as we know them are produced by a constructive synthesis imposing order on a primeval chaos, out of which both the 'objective' world and the 'subjective' mind arise. Spatial, temporal and causal order are, so to say, to be conceived as manifestations of the logical structure of all possible forms of judgement. The twelve forms of judgement correspond to the twelve categories which are expressed as *a priori* concepts, and are realized in the twelve schematisms through which orderly experience is synthesized. Synthetic *a priori* propositions express these forms of order.

> The same function which gives unity to the different representations in a judgement, gives also unity to the mere synthesis of different representations in an intuition; and this unity we call the pure conception of the understanding. . . . In this manner, there arise exactly as many pure conceptions of the understanding, applying *a priori* to objects of intuition in general, as there are logical functions in all possible judgements. . . . These conceptions we shall . . . call categories . . . [Thus to the twelve forms of judgement there correspond exactly twelve categories.] Now it is quite clear that there must be some third thing, which on the one side is homogeneous with the category, and with the phenomenon on the other, and so makes the application of the former to the latter possible. . . . (Kant, 1781, A 104–6).

These are the schematisms. Their variety must exactly match the variety of the categories and in turn of a finite set of forms of judgement. Thus the constructivist insight is constrained *a priori* by the uniqueness of the set of forms of judgement.

Does this lead to relativism? Not for Kant, since he held that there is only one system of forms of judgement manifesting itself in the structure of empirical experience, and only one *a priori* geometry and chronometry manifesting themselves in the forms of intuition, space and time. The constructivist insight, which might lead one to the thesis that the content of experience is relative to the conceptual system involved in the synthesis, is capped by the uniqueness Kant ascribes to the forms of judgement.

The constructivist insight generalized

Kant's insight, if the 'cap' were to be removed, makes room for the possibility of a radical epistemological and even ontological relativism. The thesis that combines ontological and epistemic relativism might run as follows: 'There are indefinitely many conceptual systems, each of which in application to unordered experience serves to create a world, the knowledge of which reflects that system in some fundamental way. There is no criterion for making alternative constructions for verisimilitude with respect to some one world, nor is there any way of picking out a unique body of knowledge.'

There are several contentious ideas involved in this generalization, particularly with respect to the relation between conceptual schemes and worlds. We shall examine this alleged relationship in detail in chapter 4.

Wittgenstein: The semantic insight

The meaning of words, gestures and so on, is not, so Wittgenstein demonstrates in some famous thought experiments, to be identified with the objects, which in some cases, the words or gestures signify. Words and other symbols have a meaning just insofar as they have a normatively constrained use in some human practice. The meanings of words cannot be fixed by reference to some groundwork or foundation in a fixed set of objects, even if it were the case that such a set existed. The rules for the use of words, Wittgenstein's metaphor for the normative constraints to which their use is subject, he called a 'grammar'. To engage in a common discourse the members of a community must agree in the way they use words. There must be an agreement in their 'grammar'. Grammars however, are human constructions, not super scientific theories of the world. It would seem then that they might be freely chosen, that 'grammars are autonomous'. Does this lead to relativism? Not for Wittgenstein (1953). His insight is 'capped' in the *Philosophical Investigations*.

There he remarks that not only must people agree in form of life, that is in the grammars they use, but they must also agree in judgements, that is the facts of their lives as they see them. Whatever symbolic system we choose to use whoever we are, we are a tribe of human beings, contriving to live in this world, with this inherited constitution. Grammars cannot be chosen any old way. Of course there is no one foundation on which one and only one set of semantic norms must be built, but the diversity of possible symbolic practices is constrained by nature. It is constrained not only by such a fact as that a bad choice of way of speaking about fungi may lead to death by poisoning, but also by the need, as he showed in another series of elegant thought experiments, that there should be certain natural expressions of how we are feeling, for example. There must also be certain natural capacities which can be exploited in the elementary training routines that make the acquisition of any language at all possible.

The semantic insight generalized

Some philosophers have taken Wittgenstein's insight, that the grammars of forms of life are not fixed by the way the world is, as a starting point for an argument to a radical relativism of meanings. Wittgenstein himself, so far as we can gather from his published works, did not draw any such conclusion (Conway, 1989). Every culture/language/ form of life must be grounded in the material conditions of our embodiment in just this universe. Wittgenstein uses the metaphor of the slowly changing river bed to express his muted foundationalism, with respect to the various tribal forms of life that emerge, flourish and decay within the common human form. Changes indeed there are, but meaning cannot be so labile that cultural continuity in the everyday is put in jeopardy.

Relativism in our time

In the twentieth century the challenge to absolutism can be expressed as follows: there have been denials of the Aristotelian solution to the problem posed by the anthro- pological insight; denials of the Kantian solution to the problem posed by the possibility of a variety of conceptual systems, each of which could be used to synthesize its own world, and denials of the Wittgensteinian solution to the problem posed by the insight that semantic systems are based on norms that are not abstracted directly from the nature of the world. The first appears in the claim that moral systems are various and that there is no transcen- dental moral criterion that can decide between them; the second in the claim that because the natural and human sciences have offered a sequence of comprehensive and coherent conceptual schemes, sequentially abandoned, we will never 'converge' on one that is better than all the rest; the third is manifested in the thesis that languages form closed systems of concepts.

Varieties of Relativism

We turn now to a presentation of a number of 'catalogues' of relativisms. Their diversity will serve both to cure anyone of the idea that relativism can be defended or attacked briefly and easily, or on one basis alone, and to define the complex challenge to provide an adequate exegesis and commentary on the gamut of philosophical considerations that have or could be adduced in defence of or attack upon this or that variety of relativism.

Two catalogues of relativisms

1   *By topic:*

(a)   *Semantic relativism*: Relativity of meaning to language; a word cannot be translated into another language without loss of meaning, and some words cannot be translated at all (e.g. *amae*, a Japanese word used for a unique, locally defined emotion has no equivalent in English. Its meaning can be grasped only indirectly).

(b)   *Ontological relativism*: Relativity of existence to conceptual systems: for example electric fluids existed for Franklin but not for us; witches existed for the Azande and not for us.

(c) *Moral relativism*: Relativity of moral worth to societies and epochs; sex before marriage was once held to be wrong but is not so considered now.

(d) *Aesthetic relativism*: Relativity of aesthetic value to cultures and epochs. For example the music of classical Chinese opera might well be judged cacophonous relative to the standards of Bel Canto.

2 By negation

(a) *By denying the thesis of universalism*: All people at all times and in all cultures could be brought to agree on assessment of meaningfulness, existence, goodness (moral worth) and beauty (aesthetic value) of the relevant entities. Relativist denial: No such agreement is possible.

(b) *By denying the thesis of objectivism*: assessment of meaningfulness, existence, goodness and beauty and the foundations on which they rest are capable of being presented from a point of view that is independent of the point of view of any human being in particular and of human kind in general. Relativist denial: No such point of view could exist.

(c) *By denying the thesis of foundationalism*: there is a given and permanent and only one given and permanent foundation for all assessments of meaningfulness, existence, goodness and beauty. Relativist denial: No such foundation could exist.

As we have seen the three positive or absolutist theses can be arranged in various ways, to create a range of varieties of absolutism. The strongest variety would include all three, and the weakest only the first and there are many possible combinations of intermediate strength. By negation we get three relativisms, which could also be combined in ways corresponding to those by which the variety of absolutisms is constructed. The strongest would be that created by conjoining all three denials. If we can never reach agreements, and there are no common foundations for making agreed judgements, and there is no independent point of view from which such judgements might be made, we seem to have a very strong form of relativism. Weaker varieties of relativism can be created by combining the denials in pairs with the residual absolutist thesis, and then by combining each denial with the residual pairs of absolutisms.

In this study we are concerned, for the most part, with a discussion of strong relativist theses and arguments, that is with denials of the possibility of certain kinds of assessments and judgements. The three relativisms that are defined by denial of the above three versions of absolutism are apodeictic, in that they claim that certain cognitive activities are impossible. However, the observation that as a matter of fact we human beings are not yet in a position to make universal judgements on some matter of interest, or have so far failed to find an objective foundation for the making of such judgements, is not devoid of philosophical interest. Indeed it is just that pair of conclusions that the arguments in this book seem to sustain. Against universalism there is a variety of relativism that denies that there are judgements valid in all historical conditions. Against foundationalism there is a variety of relativism that denies that there are judgements validated by reference to a single, unified body of evidence. Against objectivism there is a variety of relativism that denies that there are judgements validated by reference to an objective domain of facts.

The Shape of Anti-relativist Arguments

Paradoxes

The epistemic paradox   For any of the several varieties of relativism sketched above to be intelligible, let alone to be true, there must be some non-relativist principles that must be accepted by relativist and anti-relativist alike, if there is to be any dispute to which they can both be parties. The two most obvious are:

1.   *The thesis of ontological independence*: Entities, states, experiences and so on exist independently of culture for the fact of cultural diversity vis-à-vis these entities to show up.
2   *The thesis of transcultural intelligibility*: Descriptions of some entity, state, experience etc. must be universally intelligible, if it is to be possible to realize that the entity, state or experience being described is being treated differently in different cultures.

These theses highlight for the first time in the discussion the underlying paradox of relativism in general: in order to know that the meaning, force, ontological commitment etc. of a statement is relative to the cultural/linguistic environments in which *it* occurs, *it* must be intelligible in each of those environments to some *one* person who must make the comparison. What is the '*it*'? If it is the same statement in each cultural/linguistic environment, then there is a universally intelligible statement, that is there is at least one absolute component in human thought. If the '*it*' is merely a form of words and expresses a different statement in each cultural/linguistic environment then a relativism-revealing comparison between cultural/linguistic environments is impossible. So either relativism is false or it is unprovable.

For Goodman (1978: 22) this paradox can be circumvented. What is an argument of the sort adumbrated above supposed to do? According to Goodman a relativist is trying to convert someone to their point of view, not to explicate the nature of relativism in debate with an absolutist. It is 'Look! You can see these folk inhabit a different world from the one we do!' rather than 'Here are some premises from which the truth of relativism inexorably follows'. The latter would be paradoxical, since that relativism is true would be an absolute statement, true presumably in each cultural/linguistic environment. This issue will be pursued in more detail in chapter 2.

There is yet another way we might give content to the 'it' of the generic paradox above. Though someone who successively inhabits two cultural/linguistic environments is thereby deprived of the wherewithal to compare the acceptability of qualitatively (semantically) the same statement in each, he or she may well be aware that while some aspects of the conditions of use of the statement were different, the meaning, in some general sense, is the same. We shall develop this thought in a later chapter with the analogy of the successive understandings that a bilingual speaker could give to 'the same statement' in two different languages, despite loss of nuances. '*Crecen las palmas*' and 'The palms grow' share something we could call 'meaning', though as a line in *Guantanamera* the former has a special flavour that the latter does not share.

That there is something paradoxical about at least some varieties of relativism has been noticed by various authors.

The general form of the relativism of truth paradox runs something like this:

(I): ' "Truth is culture-bound" is true'
Either 'I' is itself culture-bound or it is not.
(a) If 'I' is culture-bound, that is if it is true, there will be some cultural settings in which it is false, or in which it cannot be formulated at all.
(b) If 'I' is not culture-bound, that is if it is false, then it will be true in all cultures.
Therefore, if 'I' is true it is false, and if it is false it is true.

Siegel (1987: 43) quotes Quine as follows: 'Truth, says the cultural relativist, is culture-bound. But if it were, then he, within his own culture, ought to see his own culture-bound truth as absolute. He cannot proclaim cultural relativism without rising above it, and he cannot rise above it without giving it up' (Quine, 1975: 313–28). When Quine tells us that cultural relativists cannot proclaim cultural relativism without paradox, it is plain that it is their own culture that must be transcended. But it does not follow from this that the relativist must rise above culture-boundedness *per se*. We can imagine a hierarchy of ever broader cultural horizons, up which a cultural relativist is driven. There may be an infinity of cultural systems. However if the regress terminates it must do so in a universal or absolute culture from which all others can be assessed. This is to give up cultural relativism. We might equally object to this conclusion from the point of view of a bilingual person whose culture-boundedness, so to say, is 'horizontal'. Such a person may well hold that he or she is committed to some culture-bound truths in English (say on the virtues of cricket as a way of building character), which are not seen as absolute because in Spanish soccer may occupy that niche (or if our bilingual comes from Extremadura, bull-fighting!).

A somewhat similar air of paradox infects some forms of epistemic relativism. This can be seen in Siegel's analysis of Hartry Field's discussion of epistemological relativism of *justified belief.* Siegel (1987: 26) quotes Field as follows:

> I understand it . . . as the doctrine that the basic epistemo-logical properties are not such properties as that of belief *B being justified,* but rather such relativized properties as that of belief *B being justified relative* to evidential system *E.* (An *evidential system* is, roughly, a bunch of rules for determin-ing under what conditions one is to believe various things); a belief is justified relative to an evidential system in certain circumstances if the rules license the belief under those circumstances (Field, 1982: 562).

But Siegel asks:

> can rival, incompatible evidential systems themselves be non-relatively or objectively or rationally evaluated? For if they can, so that we can say that *E1* is a better or superior or more justified evidential system than *E2* absolutely or non-relatively, then the relativism that Field offers is not very relativistic – for while two who hold different *E*'s can claim that their incompatible beliefs *B* and non-*B* are justified relative to their respective *E*'s, we can nevertheless judge (say) that *B* should not be believed since it is justified only relative to *E1,* which we can argue is inferior to, or less adequate than *E2.* This would reduce Field's relativism to a species of absolutism, and seems in any case to be incompatible with Field's view that epistemic values are relative – for in judging *E*'s we are after all, *evaluating E's* and such evaluating, no less than evaluating beliefs, is

epistemic evaluating and so should be relativized (to 'meta-$E's$') on Field's view. On the other hand, if rival, incompatible E's cannot be non-relatively evaluated, then it is difficult to see how any belief, no matter how bizarre, can be ruled out or evaluated negatively, for some E which will sanction it could always be constructed (Siegel, 1987: 26–27).

Again one may imagine a hierarchy of evaluating systems, up which a determined relativist is driven, step by step. Either there are infinitely many such systems or the regress ends. If it ends it ends in a final and absolute system. And this is to give up epistemic relativism.

In both cases we reach a dilemma. Either no judgement is final or there are absolute judgements. Neither horn suits the relativist book.

The moral paradox   Moral relativism is the thesis that a principle is moral only in so far as it is mandatory, and principles are only mandatory relative to some particular moral system, and there is no universal moral system. *If this is itself a moral principle [and some may insist that it is not] then it must be mandatory in all moral systems, contrary to the basic thesis. Or there is another moral system, which is supervenient to all other moral systems. In which case the list of moral systems in the formulation of the first thesis does not include all moral systems. A further twist to this paradox has been given by Berlin (Gray, 1994), in denying that there are any coherent moral systems.

Transcendental arguments

If it can be established that there are necessary conditions for the possibility of experience, for the possibility of language etc. then these would be universal, that is they must obtain in all cultures in which relativism, in whatever form, can be formulated. This move to a mild absolutism would be undermined if it were conceded that the very idea of a transcendental argument is culture dependent. Such a concession has been shadowed forth in some of the writings of radical feminists for whom even Aristotelian logic is a device by which white, middle-class, Western males preserve their hegemony. We do not propose to address that thesis here. Indeed we are unable to do so, since our only tools for addressing such theses are rooted in the principles of logic. Instead we shall turn to the task of setting out the bare bones of some relevant transcendental arguments.

The general form of a transcendental argument runs something as follows:

1   We cannot experience the absence of experience, nor state the non-existence of language.
2   There are necessary conditions for the possibility of experience and for the usability and meaningfulness of language.
3   From 1) and 2) these conditions must hold for any universe in which there is experience and language.

Kant puts forward in a famous argument that there are certain necessary conditions for the possibility of experience that must obtain in any universe in which there is experience. But our attention will be focused on transcendental arguments for the necessary conditions for the possibility of language. Holiday (1988) has argued that there are grounds for setting up transcendental arguments relative to the possibility of language implicit in the later writings of Wittgenstein.

If language is necessary to culture then these necessary conditions will be required for there to be any culture, and therefore will be universal for all cultures. There seem to be two classes of such conditions:

1   A transcendental pragmatic condition as noticed by Wittgenstein (1953): there must be language like precursors in order that language should be possible. It is only because there are natural expressions for some of our bodily feelings, for instance the natural expression of pain, that can serve as necessary precursors for the use of a public language to express our private feelings. We first use verbal expressions, for example 'Oh! Such a pain' as a substitute for the natural expressions. There must be natural regularities in form of life in order for the 'artificial' regularities of rule-following to take root. Without the capacity to grasp the import of a rule language use would be impossible.
2   A cluster of moral conditions as argued for by Holiday (1988): for example there must be interpersonal trust for language use to be possible. If there were no place in the culture for the practice of truth-telling, the most elementary institution of mutual trust, language could never be established. It must be possible for us to have the idea that someone means what they say.

We shall return to develop these arguments in later chapters.

Our Argumentative Strategy

We have identified four varieties of relativism by topic. These are semantic, epistemic, ontological and valuational (moral and aesthetic) relativism. Taking each variety in turn we shall set out arguments for and against relativism in each context. We shall attempt to interpret the upshot of the dialectic of these debates within the framework of the three varieties of absolutism that we have identified: namely, universalism, objectivism and foundationalism. In no case do we think that we have found arguments of overwhelming strength on either side of the debate. Perhaps there is no final resolution in rational terms of this great schism in people's attitudes to existence, knowledge, meaning and values.

The arguments will be fought out in terms of an unchallenged but unanalysed notion of truth. But as Margolis (1991) has pointed out there is an 'alethic' challenge to absolutisms as well as an epistemic one. Assuming 'truth' the Protagorean sceptic relativizes knowledge to each individual knower. It is to that version of epistemic relativism that we shall devote our critical attention in chapter 3. Finally, in the last chapter, we shall return to examine, in the light of some recent writings by Margolis, the deepest of all issues, that of alethic relativism, the thesis that the strict 'true/false' dichotomy may not apply to all judgements in all contexts of enquiry.

2

Semantic Relativism

Introduction

The first arguments for relativism that we shall examine in detail are those clustered around the problems of meaning in relation to the fact of the diversity of languages. We shall encounter the issue of meaning again in another range of arguments, those that cluster around the relativity of meanings to world views or paradigms.

According to semantic relativism the meanings of words are functions of their places in particular languages, each of which expresses and is constitutive of a unique cultural complex. Though translation is possible between languages, it is always and necessarily incomplete and therefore revisable.

It is now commonplace to regard languages as sets of tools which can be used for a variety of purposes. This insight displaces the traditional idea that all words are really names. From St Augustine to Russell theorists have tried to understand language as if it were mainly used for labelling objects of various kinds. Where a label seems to exist without any obvious object suitable surrogates have been invented, leading to intractable philosophical problems. If the meanings of words lie in their uses, and these uses are multiple and diverse, then we need some other model than the proper name and the pointing finger to capture the inwardness of meaning. We shall see that one important anti-relativist position depends on the thesis that words are names and falls with it. Following the 'tool' metaphor we shall work with the principle that language serves people as a means for accomplishing a variety of tasks. It is used for labelling things, for drawing attention to interesting or important situations in the environment, for expressing how we feel, for issuing orders, for expressing preferences, for issuing invitations, for sealing commitments and so on. In this chapter we shall arrange our exposition of the arguments for the relevant variety of relativism around the distinction between languages in use as devices for describing and explaining natural phenomena, and languages in use as devices for accomplishing social acts. In the former case we shall concentrate on utterances taken as statements of fact and subject to assessment as true or false. In the latter case we shall concentrate on utterances taken as expressions of social acts subject to assessment according to criteria of social effectiveness.

We shall first examine two anti-relativist positions, each arguing for the possibility of establishing universal meanings, though in very different ways. We have already argued that 'Relativism' is not univocal. Varieties of relativism emerge by denial of three root absolutisms; universalism, objectivism and foundationalism. In the matter of meanings the three 'opposites' come out as follows: universalism, there are meanings which are preserved in translations from any language into all languages; objectivism, there are meanings which are fixed by matters independent of human beliefs and interests; and foundationalism, there is a basic set of elementary units of meaning from which the meanings of all lexical items can be built.

We shall begin our examination of the arguments for and against semantic relativism by a critical exposition of two absolutist positions. One depends on the 'all words are names' principle, and opposes relativism with a defence of a foundationalist account of meaning. The other depends on a principle of perfect translatability for a certain minimal vocabulary, and opposes relativism with a universalist account of meaning. There have been objectivist accounts of meaning, Plato's theory of forms as an account of the meaning of property words, for example, but we shall not discuss that view in any detail.

Turning to arguments directed positively to support semantic relativism we shall highlight first some alleged problems of translation that tend to support relativism. These problems have been discussed by W. V. Quine (1969). We shall find that much of the criticism of Quine's thesis has turned on his views about the nature of psychology. Quine's arguments are rooted in a primitive behaviourism, disputed by most of his critics, such as Davidson and others. However the upshot of the debate is neither clear nor conclusive. A second line of argument that tends towards relativism can be found in the writings of Waismann, an argument that owes a good deal to Wittgenstein. Languages are independent, mutually closed, symbolic systems for the performance of all kinds of tasks, including describing and explaining phenomena, as these are revealed in the investigations of the natural sciences. Their constitutive role in the formation of distinctive lifeworlds is, it is argued, enough to require the admission of at least some measure of relativism of meanings.

Absolutist Accounts of Meaning

Meaning as object signified: all words are names

According to the theory of language developed by Wittgenstein (1922) in his *Tractatus Logico-Philosophicus* the elementary units of language are simple names the meaning of which are the elementary objects they signify. These elementary names acquire meaning by being correlated with an object. We could picture the process of meaning giving as rather like baptism, a ceremonial act by which a name and a person are permanently joined by convention. All this is 'in principle' for Wittgenstein, since he was unable to give an account of the elementary units either of the language or of the world. However if the world does consist of an ordered array of elementary objects, and the elementary signs of the language are the names of these objects, meanings must be universal, objective and foundational. For there to be determinate sense, he argues, there must be simple objects. There could be no fundamental problems about translation from one language to another. Since the English word 'glass' and the Castillian word '*vaso*' denote the same thing, they must have the same meaning. Sentences (as ordered collections of names) are structured by a universal grammar, logic. States of affairs (as ordered collections of objects) are structured isomorphically to sentences. Hence absolute truth conceived as a perfect correspondence between arrays of elementary names and arrays of elementary objects, is possible.

If we were to accept this account of meaning as object signified and of truth as correspondence, with respect to a world of stable and elementary objects, then we would have reached a very strong form of semantic absolutism. Meanings, as definite material entities, would be universal, objective and foundational.

Arguments against meaning as object signified

In order that the act of pointing to an object should work as a device for establishing meaning, some 'stage setting' is required, that is a place must be prepared for a new word. For example should I wish to establish the meaning of the word 'cerise' by pointing to something I must be able to make clear that it is the colour of the object that I am referring to, rather than its shape, texture or some other perceptible property. We have to somehow make clear under which determinable, in this case *colour*, our new determinate, 'cerise', is to fall. Is 'glass' a word for a kind of object or a kind of stuff? Would we translate it into Castillian as '*vaso*' or '*cristal*'?

The fact that objects are indefinitely complex means that even the disambiguation we can achieve by stage-setting can never be final. No sequence of acts of pointing (ostension) can guarantee that there will be no borderline cases which the original or exemplary cases, used to fix the meaning by 'baptismal' ceremony, do not quite fit.

If we try to recover the primordial simplicity of such cases as the giving of a proper name to a person, by reverting to elementary subjective sensations as the meaning giving objects, then each person would have their own private meanings for their words, meanings which could never be coordinated with those of another person, since there can be no public access to private sensations. No public language would be possible. But there is a still more damning consequence yet of this idea. There would be no surety even for the private linguist that his or her words meant the same today as they did at other times, since subjective, private sensations are ephemeral. How would one judge whether today's sensation was like yesterday's, and therefore whether today's meaning was the same as yesterday's? It is no good saying that one remembers the sensations of the past. How do we know that we are remembering them correctly? The fact that we can and do talk meaningfully about how we feel is used by Wittgenstein in his Private Language Argument (Wittgenstein, 1953: 263–319) as yet another reason for abandoning the idea that the meanings of words are the objects that they signify. Naming will not do as a universal account of meaning.

There is a further assumption in the background of the meaning theory we have been discussing. If it is to be plausible it must be possible to pick out the relevant objects and properties prior to the establishment of the appropriate words of which they will come to be the meanings. But in many cases the objects only become accessible when we have mastered the relevant concept, that is can use the relevant word. Learning the word and learning to identify the object, so to say, go together. This is evident in the way we learn scientific vocabularies, for instance botanical and zoological classifications. Our ability to discriminate ash from elm is acquired in the course of learning the correct uses of the words 'ash' and 'elm'.

Closely related to the referential theory of the meaning of words is the truth-conditions theory of the meaning of statements. According to this view the meaning of a statement is the set of conditions which would verify it. This idea is a descendent of the more general thesis that a statement is meaningful only if it is possible to describe the conditions under which it would be accepted or rejected, verified or falsified. From this commonsense idea it was not difficult to slip into thinking that meaning would be found in truth-conditions for the statement in question.

When applied to the discourse of the sciences the theory runs into immediate and fatal difficulties. For example no general law-like statement of the form 'All As are B' would be meaningful on a strict application of the theory, since such a statement is meant to comprehend not only observed and unobserved actual cases, but possible cases too. The truth-conditions for such a statement could never be complete, and so neither could its meaning.

There are many statements in the discourses of science that describe unobservable states and processes. Theoretical statements must be tested for truth by testing some of their logical consequences. The truth-conditions for statements about atoms are to be found, for example, in the regularities with which different masses of elementary substances combine with one another. But if the meanings were the truth-conditions we should be obliged to confine the meanings of theoretical statements to some function of their observable consequences. This would run contrary to the widely held belief that scientific theories which describe the unobservable or hidden mechanisms that produce the phenomena we observe can be assessed for the degree to which they are true. This belief is called 'scientific realism'.

Neither the meanings of general or theoretical terms seem to be accounted for by reference to a foundation in objective exemplars. The meaning of theoretical terms like 'natural selection' and 'force field' seem to emerge from complex patterns of metaphor. The upshot of these diverse considerations of the language of science requires us to reject semantic absolutism in its objectivist and foundationalist manifestations. But it still might be true that there is a universal vocabulary into which the diverse vocabularies of all human languages can be translated. It is important to see this as a species of the generic concept of universalism that we introduced in chapter 1. There could be beliefs which hold good in all contexts, at all times, and for all persons, only if the language in which such a belief would have to be expressed could be translated into some universal vocabulary and syntax.

The Argument for a Universal Root Vocabulary

The relativity of meanings of the items in many word classes to local cultures, along both historical and anthropological dimensions of diversity, is well established (Lutz, 1988). Does this necessitate the adoption of a thorough-going relativism with respect to meanings? Anna Weirzbicka (1992) has claimed that there is a small number of words for which exact equivalents exist in all languages and in every culture. These words, if they existed, would provide a 'bridgehead', by the use of which, from a position in any language whatever, a linguistic equivalent for any word in another language system could be constructed. There are two parts to this thesis: that the basic universal vocabulary does indeed exist, and that it can be used to reach into each and every language to construct the meaning of the rest of the vocabulary of that language in terms of another.

According to Wierzbicka there are about ten universal concepts the linguistic expressions for which are perfectly translatable into all known human languages. The two most plausible candidates are expressed in the English words 'I' and 'this'. If this were the case it would follow that any human language could serve as the universal metalanguage into which all other language could be translated, since the ten concepts will be realized in each language in a set of words, mutually translatable into all others. Wierzbicka does not present an argument for her claim. She simply asserts it. Her claim seems to be that this universal minimum vocabulary is a 'matter of fact'. If this were the case an argument against her thesis and therefore for relativism could be built by showing, case by case, that these words were not perfectly translatable into all human languages. Remember that the point is not whether the use of a similar expression in another language culture can be explained in English, but that there is an exact equivalent to the pronoun 'I', the demonstrative 'this' and so on, in all other known languages. We shall not undertake a wholesale refutation of the Wierzbicka anti–relativist thesis, but confine ourselves to the case of the first person pronoun 'I'. Since the idea that there is a universal means for speakers to refer to themselves seems the most plausible of Wierzbicka's candidates, a thorough discussion of 'I' will be sufficient for our purposes. In this discussion we shall be focusing on language in its role as an instrument for social action, rather than as a means for recording and conveying information.

The role of pronouns and indexical inflexions in speaking

We shall be analysing language-in-use in terms of the speech-act as the functional unit. An example will help to introduce the notion. When a judge sentences a convicted prisoner in such terms as 'You are to serve seven years in solitary confinement' the judge's utterance does not describe the future state of the felon, but enforces it. The judge's utterance, so considered, is the performance of a speech-act. Analysis of linguistic features of speech-acts, such as the role of pronouns in their formulation, requires attention to more than the overt structure of the sentence that has been used. One must identify the social act that has been performed. In its capacity to perform a social act an utterance is said to have illocutionary force in context. We shall take it for granted that the force of an utterance is the joint product of the speaker's intention as this is displayed in what has been said, and the uptake of the person or persons to whom it has been addressed, as displayed in the utterances and actions with which they respond to the speech-act. The gaolers drag the prisoner away. The prisoner begs for mercy and so on. If all that and more happens then the judge's utterance is indeed effective as an act of sentencing. We shall now try to show that the English pronoun 'I' is not fully translatable into all languages, nor can the first person devices of many languages be fully translated as 'I'.

In all languages which possess those useful devices, pronouns serve two major functions. In the third person they tie the narrative to a common referent. Thus we can say 'John brought home the cake and he divided it among the hungry children'. 'He' is literally a pro-noun standing for 'John', just as 'it' stands in for 'cake'. Each noun-pronoun pair are coreferential. This is the anaphoric use of pronouns. But in the first and second person pronouns have a very different function. They are not pro-nouns at all. They are indexicals.

The term 'indexical' has been used in several ways in the literature. For the purpose of a comparative study of the uses of the first person across cultures the fact that knowledge of the occasion of utterance is necessary for the hearer to complete the sense of an indexical expression is not the most important feature of the use of indexicals. It is true that someone only knows to whom the pronoun 'I' refers in a certain context if they were present and attentive on the occasion of that utterance. This is the focus of Jakobson's (1957) 'shifter' account of first and second person pronoun use. The reference shifts with each occasion of use. But for our purposes pronouns are best looked on as ways of using the known location of the speaker to index the empirical content and illocutionary force of speech-acts with that location. So if someone says 'I can see the procession' we know that the procession is visible from the bodily location of the speaker. 'I' is used in much the same way as latitude and longitude are used to index statements about cities, lakes and so on with their locations on the abstract geographical grid. The grid of spatial locations is the array of embodied speakers (Muhl-hausler and Harré, 1991).

It is easy to show that the first person cannot be normally used anaphorically, that is as a stand-in for a noun or proper name. The utterance of 'Rom and Michael will sort the luggage' commits the speaker to nothing. It might have the illocutionary force of an order. But 'We will sort the luggage' commits the speakers to carrying out that useful task. It has the illocutionary force of a promise. This distinction holds even if it was one of Rom or Michael who issued the first utterance.[1]

There is another way of bringing out the point. The use of a proper name like 'Fred' is almost wholly dependent on referential relations established in some sort of baptismal rite with a being that lies outside the discourse. Its referent (its 'deictic anchor') is a person. The role of first person pronouns as 'deictic anchors' is different from the way proper names work. 'Fred' refers directly to him whose name it is, but first and second person pronouns tie the discourse to this or that human being only indirectly. In the same way a geodesic reference ties an utterance to an island only via the grid of lines of latitude and longitude. 'The treasure is buried at 33N and 23W' is helpful only to those adventurers who are familiar with the abstract system of geodesy. Similarly a first person pronoun is effective only for those persons who are familiar with the location of the speaker in the array of embodied persons.

If the role of pronouns is taken to be locative, in the manner we suggest, we shall show that on any occasion of use a first person pronoun is multiply indexical. As we have seen it serves to index the content of a speech-act with the spatial location of the embodied speaker. But it is also indexical of locations in other manifolds. For example the illocutionary force of a first person utterance, say its force as a complaint, is indexed with the moral and social locations of the speaker. How that complaint is taken will depend on what the habits of the speaker are ('a right whiner') and what right they have to make the complaint ('a disgruntled customer').

We shall work with the hypothesis that our usage of first and second person indexical devices (many of which are pronouns) is dominated by four manifolds:

1 *A spatial manifold*, consisting of a discrete set of spatial locations carved out of the continuous manifold of physical space by the spatially located bodies of the relevant speaker/speaker groups.
2 *A temporal manifold*, consisting of a discrete set of temporal moments carved out of the continuous manifold of physical time by the actual moments of utterance of those speech-actions from which speech-acts will be created by speaker/speaker uptake.
3 *A 'moral manifold'* representing the array of person-types in the local moral order, defined by the speaker's

moral standing (reliable, dishonest, careless, etc.) vis-à-vis that of the counter speaker and others in the relevant community. The manifold of 'moral locations' consists of the shifting and multiple patterns of positions that conversants occupy relative to one another.

4 *A 'social' manifold*, a set of social positions, which speaker could occupy vis-à-vis counter speaker and others in the relevant community.

We shall develop these concepts somewhat in illustrating our thesis. At this point we need to introduce the concept of a fully enriched language. In such a language the empirical content and illocutionary force of all first and second person utterances would be fully indexed with the speaker's and interlocutors' locations in all four manifolds by means of the use of the appropriate pronoun or functionally equivalent inflexion.

We can use the concept of a 'fully enriched language' to test Wierzbicka's thesis concerning the perfect translatability of the English 'I' into all known languages. If 'I' can be translated into all languages then only if the first person devices of all these languages can be back translated into English, could English serve as the universal meta-language of Wierzbicka's theory, and so as the language for the discussion of personhood across the gamut of human patterns of life. In a 'fully enriched language' the pronoun system or its functional equivalent is capable of being used to index the content and the illocutionary force of all utterances with the locations of the persons engaged in a conversation in all four manifolds. Since there is at least one language in which pronouns index speaker locations in each of the four manifolds, comparison of the indexical possibilities of any one language with those we have assigned to the 'fully enriched language' will be a test for perfect translatability. The thesis of perfect translatability will fail if there are no known languages in which the first person is indexical of the location in all four manifolds.

A comparison of actual languages with the fully enriched language

So far as one is able to ascertain, all known languages have devices for indexing the content of utterances with the speaker's spatial location. Since the place of utterance is identical with the location of the body of the speaker one might be tempted to think that the link between person as speaker and his or her body, implicit in the use of the first person, was necessarily one to one. This is certainly a feature of non–pathological uses of the English 'I'. However Dorothy Lee's (1950) studies of Wintu indexicals reveals that the tight link between singular embodiment, spatial location and the singularity of personhood expressed in first person indexicals may not be universal. For instance *-da* is the Wintu singular first person indexical. In certain circumstances it can be used to index the content of an utterance with the location of more than one body. Thus *lime-da* is rendered as 'I am ill' but *tuhutum-lim-tca-da*, which we perforce must render as 'My mother is ill', should run more like 'The compound body of mummy and me is where illness resides'. The infix *-tca-* indicates the spatial diffusion of the *-da* index. This is not a perfect translation but a necessary compromise, since *-tca-da* is not 'we', nor does the possessive 'me' in the above 'translation' correspond to anything in Wintu.

We conclude that the Wierzbicka thesis as regards the spatial indexicality of the first person is false. '-*da*' cannot be translated without remainder by English 'I'.

English pronouns are not inflected for time of utterance relative to the temporal aspects of the content of the utterance. The temporal indexicality of a speech-act, that is, the temporal relations of the content and the illocutionary force of an utterance to its moment of utterance, are fixed through tenses of verbs, and special temporal indexicals like 'now', together with certain uses of 'when'. However in Kawi (Becker and Oka, 1974) pronouns are sensitive to the relative temporal location of the moment of utterance and the temporal properties of content and illocutionary force.

Kawi pronouns are built out of three elements, a locative, spatial and/or temporal index *i*- and/or *nga*-, a deictic formative (-*k*-) and a person index (-*i*,-*a*,-*u*). Thus *i-k-i* would be read 'me-there (distant)' or 'me-past (distant)' depending on context. However if a contrast is needed between an index of a distant place and an index of a distant time, *nga-k-i* is used to index time only. Since English pronouns do not index utterances with times, Kawi first person forms cannot be translated without reminder by English 'I'.

Local and contextual knowledge is needed to understand spatio–temporal indexing. Indexing a speech-act with respect to a moral order, for example, the taking of responsibility by indexing the illocutionary force of one's speech-act with one's location in a moral order is more complex. Moral orders are subject to moment by moment transformation. To understand this we need to introduce a relatively new analytical concept, 'positioning' (Hollway, 1984). A 'position' (or in Goffman's terminology a 'footing') in conversation is a set of rights, duties and obligations that a person may be ascribed or take up as to the types of speech-acts they can be taken to have produced jointly with the other conversants. In particular the illocutionary forces that are available to speakers in some local moral order are constrained by the 'positions' such speakers occupy. Thus a person, positioned as a caretaker, has the right to offer advice to someone positioned as one in need of care. The speech-actions of the former can become the basis of jointly constructed speech-acts having that illocutionary force. The story-line or narrative convention that structures the sequence of such speech-acts into a conversation will also be sensitive to the positions ascribed or adopted and the illocutionary forces of the speech-acts created jointly by the conversants. Thus if two people are positioned as 'nurse' and 'patient' their subsequent actions should conform to the story-line 'being ill and being taken care of'.

The structure of this mutual influence can be expressed in the 'positioning triangle':

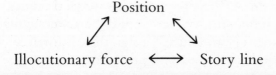

These 'elements' are so related that each is involved in making the others more or less determinate. Thus only relative to an acknowledged position are the illocutionary forces of speech-actions made determinate as speech-acts, and the unfolding sequence of speech-acts combined to form a coherent conversation, intelligible as the living out of some narrative. Positions, illocutionary forces and story lines shift with respect to one another. It is easy to see that one and the same sequence of speech-actions can be the basis for an indefinite number of simultaneous conversations (Sabat and Harré, 1992). Indexing speech-acts with illocutionary force must depend on the positions that are taken to exist in the context.

So far as we can tell all languages have a device for indexing speech-acts with speaker responsibility. But these devices can be complex, and hierarchical. In Spanish there is a great difference between the illocutionary force of an utterance with only the first person inflexion of the verb, and the force of the same words prefixed with '*Yo*'.

The cultural variations we find in this dimension are of some importance for the test of the Wierzbicka thesis. Is the illocutionary force of an utterance taken up as a speech-act indexed with speaker's responsibility or with responsibility of speaker's reference group? In Japanese, on those occasions when explicit indexicals are used, it seems clearly to be the latter. In much spoken Japanese pronouns do not appear. Indexicality is achieved contextually. We do not think it helpful to imagine some ghost pronouns, understood in the discourse. It is more in keeping with the ethnography of Japanese everyday discourse to interpret the absence of pronouns as a sign that the discourse is only weakly indexical, and that pronouns are a marked usage. For instance the word *uchi* ('my house') is in common use as a first person indexical marking the utterance with a commitment by speaker's family (Bachnik, 1982). Similarly if *watakushi* and *watashi* are used these are marked usages, in which the illocutionary force of an utterance is indexed with the social locations of the speaker, that is with locations in the manifold of social positions expressible in the fully enriched 'language'. Our informants told us that *boku*, a relative newcomer to the Japanese register of first person indexicals, is used when one wishes to appear as 'one of the boys' but knows in one's heart that one is really superior. We are also told that this is now the pronoun of choice for indexically marked first person utterances by feminists. The pronoun ore has an interesting role, since we believe that it is used to detach the normal illocutionary force of the unmarked utterance from either the moral or social manifold of person positions. By way of contrast it is clear that neither English nor Inuit have the resources to index utterances with the social positions of speaker/hearer. In French, German, Spanish and other European languages this indexing is done with complex and language specific variations on the second and third person, for example in French 'tu' and 'vous'. In no European languages is such indexing capable of being done with the first person pronoun.

We must conclude then that in this respect too, Wierzbicka's thesis is false. Japanese first person pronouns cannot be rendered without remainder by the English 'I', since there is no pronoun in Japanese which does not index a speech-act with the social position of speaker, vis-a-vis hearer or counter-speaker.

The failure of Wierzbicka's thesis for indexicals does not, of course, entail that it must fail for all the words in her list of English candidates for perfect translatability. Nor does it entail that the uses of indexical devices in an alien language/culture cannot be described in another language, or their locative implications rendered in some other way. It does entail that the several devices of systems that are alien to English cannot be reconstituted in a universal metalanguage, though we have just explained the force of Japanese pronouns. But we cannot linguistically reconstitute Japanese life in English. The semantic theses under consideration here are not about understanding another culture/language, but about translating it, that is reproducing it in the other linguistic system. However, since 'I' was the best candidate for a role in a universal metalanguage, its failure casts doubt on Wierzbicka's other candidates.

If the claim that there is a universal vocabulary is refuted does this entail the other versions of the absolutist thesis need not be considered? If there are no universal 'words' there could still be a basic vocabulary, that is there might be words in each language which would serve as the definitional tool for all and every concept in that language. Though universalism might fail, it might be that each language rests on its own unique foundation.

The Upshot of These Arguments

The claim that seemed to be implicit in the analysis of language set out in Wittgenstein's *Tractatus* is very strong. If we were to accept it we would be led to an absolutist view of meaning as universal, objective and foundational. But the arguments we developed against it showed only that meaning is neither objective nor foundational, that is cannot be identified with a set of elementary extra-linguistic objects. However the refutation of the Wierzbicka thesis, which involved a strong claim for universalism, but for a somewhat narrower range of words, showed that for the best candidate class, namely indexicals, meanings are not universal. Taking the two arguments together we have shown that meaning is neither universal, objective nor foundational. Meanings are not fixed everywhere and for all time by a set of basic objects, nor are there universal meanings to be found among other classes of words than nouns. If semantic absolutism fails to what degree are we now driven to accept semantic relativism? We now turn to positive arguments for some relativist theses.

Arguments for Semantic Relativism

The 'radical translation thesis'

Among the writings of W. V. Quine there is a series of arguments concerning translation that can be recruited to the defence of Semantic Relativism, though Quine makes use of them for rather different purposes. The arguments are somewhat elusive, so we will begin by quoting Hookway's (1988) elegant summary:

> Quine's argument rests upon his view of which psychological facts are relevant to the correctness of a translation manual. He distinguishes cases where our preference for one manual over another results from our seeing that only the first fits the facts, from cases where, on pragmatic grounds, we prefer one manual to another when both fit the facts equally well. There could be alternative manuals each of which fits the facts perfectly. He allows for two distinct bases of choice between translation manuals: whether manuals respect the truth about stimulus meanings; and how far they meet pragmatic standards of charity[2] and the like (Hookway, 1988).

Quine's believes that there is something about the nature of meaning that, properly understood, shows the impossibility of effecting a perfect translation, sentence by sentence, from one language to another, relying on linguistic facts alone. He imagines the translator concocting and trying to make use of various translation manuals, in each of which the words of one language are matched to their putative correlates in the other language. If we set aside considerations of utility then, he argues, in principle there are an indefinite number of different translation manuals, for any pair of languages, which will legitimate sets of alternative sentences, one for each manual, which fit the facts equally well, and between which no matter of fact can decide.

Of course the force of this claim will depend on what 'linguistic meaning' is supposed to be and what is to count as the kind of 'fact' that might be advanced in attempting to decide between alternative manuals. The answers to these queries turn out to be physicalistic, individualistic and positivistic. The argument assumes that words in descriptive discourses are used to refer to physical objects. It rests on the thought that physical objects are indefinitely complex, rich in alternative aspects. And that the 'stimulus meaning' of descriptive words is such that there will always remain alternative aspects which might have been meant by the user of such a word. In real cases we do manage to pick a preferred translation, but to cite that observation in contention with Quine's thesis, is to miss the point. The question is not which manual is the most useful but which is true. It is that which can never be determined, so the argument runs. The argument is simple: stimulus meaning can never be guaranteed to be in one to one correspondence with that aspect of a physical state of affairs to which a speaker refers on a particular occasion. So if all we can translate are stimulus meanings the question of their referents always remains open. What is this stimulus meaning? It is the pattern of electromagnetic impulses that fall on the retina of the subject. The same pattern of electromagnetic impulses will fall on the eye of someone who takes 'chicken' to refer to a whole and unitary domestic bird and someone who takes it to refer to a characteristic assemblage of feathers, wings, beak and so on. To the obvious objection that differences in point of reference will emerge in further discourse Quine has seemed indifferent, reiterating the point that no matter how far a discourse would extend, the essential gap between stimulus meaning and intended referent will remain.

It is clear that the argument for indeterminacy of translation splits linguistic matters into two categories, the intentional character of individual thought, which must on Quine's thesis remain forever opaque, and the extensional character of common descriptions which can depend only on stimulus meaning, the commonalities of which allegedly come from physical science. This distinction rests wholly on Quine's Machian scientism. According to Quine (1975:2):

> Science itself teaches that there is no clairvoyance; that the only information that can reach our sensory surfaces from external objects must be limited to two-dimensional optical projections and various impacts of air waves on the eardrums and some gaseous reactions of the nasal passages . . . How, the challenge proceeds, could one hope to find out about the external world from such meagre traces? In short, if our science were true, how could we know it? (Quine, 1975:2).

This kind of scientism and the paradox it engenders was what prompted Goethe's response to Newton's *Opticks*. The point had already been made by Locke. There can be no physicalist account of why one surface looks red and another white, even if we knew all about the atomic structure of the surfaces. Yet it is just as much a fact of the matter that the one looks red and the other white as it is that one has this structure and the other that. (Perhaps, given the heavy theoretical burden borne by hypotheses of atomic structure it is more so.) Why is it less a fact about the world that pomegranates are red when ripe and tubas noisy when blown than that 'red' light has a wavelength of about 6,000 Å, and that the amplitude of a sound wave is proportional to the energy of the disturbance?

We can follow the slipping and sliding of a typical Machian reductionism in the following (Quine, 1969: 167):

> Mental states and events do not reduce to behaviour, nor are they explained by behaviour. [Thus something's looking red to someone is not reducible to what they do or tend to do, say selecting a fruit from a dish.] They are explained by neurology, when they are explained. . . . When we talk of mental states or events subject to behavioral criteria, we can rest assured that we are not just bandying words; there is a physical fact of the matter, a fact ultimately of elementary physical states. [Thus someone's seeing red is reducible to (explained by? correlated with?) some physical state.] (Quine, 1969:167)

Taken all in all we seem to be presented with a curious situation. If we wish to translate the descriptive vocabulary of one language into another we can succeed just in so far as we can assign stimulus meanings to the words. Residual differences, which may be profound, can be only in what those words mean to the current user. But in the light of the remarks above about the explanatory power of neurology, the residual personal or cultural meanings must be differentially accessible via neurophysiology. And so in the end we could attain to a definite translation.

But the Machian point of view is itself fatally flawed in a way which undercuts the 'naturalistic' resolution which one can draw out of the whole Quinean corpus. There would be no way to identify a neural state or process as that which was relevant to a given mental event if all we had with which to identify and individuate that state or process were neurological criteria. The familiar Taxonomic Priority Thesis requires the independent intelligibility of the ordinary languages with which we describe the world and ourselves. Only if we already know what 'remembering' is could we look for whatever neurological mechanisms are engaged in the processes by which someone remembers. The discovery of these mechanisms no more licenses the elimination of the ordinary language criteria for the use of the word remembering, than the realization that tennis must be played with rackets eliminates the concepts of 'foot fault', 'ball out' and so on from our account of a game. *Ordinary language has taxonomic priority in the classification of body parts and their behaviours as relevant to anything psychological.*

Quine himself does not admit to relativism. On the contrary. The upshot of the radical translation thesis for him is the excision of all that is relative, namely personal meanings, from the only ontology that he takes seriously, the ontology of 'science'. But since his view depends crucially on Machian positivism, and that philosophy of science is hopelessly inadequate, Radical Translation, shorn of its scientistic and positivist accompaniments, is strongly relativist. If we reject Quine's philosophy of science, which we must, we cannot have recourse to electro-molecular goings on as the guarantors of extrapersonal stabilities of stimulus meanings. These can retrieve, at best, the subjective, private personal experiences someone may have on using a word. That, as has famously been pointed out, could never serve as a reliable grounding for word meanings.

To complete the examination of 'Quinean' relativism we shall sketch a telling criticism, which in our view amounts to a refutation of the thesis. Evans (1982) draws a distinction between a theory of meaning, which purports to explain people's linguistic dispositions, and a translation manual, which purports to give linguistic equivalents between languages. The fact that no one can ever be quite sure that he or she has grasped the personal meanings someone else attaches to their words, even in listening to a member of one's own tribe, is of no great significance unless it undercuts the possibility of formulating theories about the local or personal significance that the members of another tribe attach to their descriptive vocabulary.

Suppose in setting up a translation manual for rendering Spanish into English we run across a new word, let it be '*vergüenza*', which we notice that Spaniards use when we would be inclined to use the English word 'shame'. Stimulus meaning, in Quine's sense, let us suppose, is the same, that is these words are used in what appear to be similar circumstances, according to some physicalist criterion of similarity. The radical translation thesis says that the personal or tribal meaning with which this word is used by Spaniards may still be different from that with which 'shame' is used by the English speaker, and that we could never know this since there is no Quinean 'fact of the matter'. Evans's argument is simple but devastating. We can express one theory of Spanish usage in 'Axiom A' in which we suppose that '*vergüenza*' is the word for the feeling associated with having been seen to commit an immoral act, which would tie it tightly to English 'shame' in our translation manual. We could have another theory expressed in 'Axiom B', in which we suppose that '*vergüenza*' is the word for the feeling of being seen to behave ridiculously. Remember that our Spaniard displays *vergüenza* when caught in a situation, say shoplifting, in which our Englishman would display what we would call 'shame', that is they both blush and squirm. We now proceed to consider an 'Axiom' for the English phrase 'ridiculous behaviour' as applied to Spanish life. We find that it includes, in its 'stimulus meaning' tripping over one's own feet and being caught shoplifting. Thus 'A Spaniard will not display what Spaniards would call *"vergüenza"* when tripping over his/her own shoe laces' will get the 'stimulus meaning' wrong. And, of course, we can repeat this procedure indefinitely often, to deal with each doubt as it arises.

So even if, as we must, we reject the scientism and positivism of Quine's way of dealing with the incipient relativism of 'Radical Translation', Evans provides a procedure by which any given translation manual can be indefinitely improved. This would seem to weaken the relativist conclusion drawn from Radical Translation. Each time we suspect that we may be 'out of line' in our use of an expression, we can formulate a testable theory to check. Bernard Harrison has drawn our attention to an interpretation of Quine's line on meaning that dispenses with any idea of 'what was really meant' as that which can never be known for sure by the foreigner. According to that interpretation there is nothing that we do not know that we could know. Translation manuals can only be ranked pragmatically, roughly by how well they might help us to 'get by' in the market place. This does not take us back to the Evans's position, since that is built around the idea of indefinite improvement, which presupposes that there is something we could come to know that we do not know.

Meaning as a function of context

If a significant 'part' of the meaning of linguistic items is contributed by the context of use, and every context of use is unique in some relevant way, then there must be an irreducibly relativist element in meaning. If context does play such a role, sentences/words could not be moved freely from context to context with unchanged meanings. We are skirting a deep philosophical issue in expressing ourselves thus. What are the criteria of identity for sentences/words and so on, that we can talk of them being transported from context to context? We shall shelve this problem for the moment. At first glance the relativist claim seems plainly exaggerated. Surely one can use the word 'saw' in any number of carpenters' shops, logging camps and hardware stores, and mean the same thing by it. And what about the word we use for expressing the fact that we have seen something yesterday?

We can begin the construction of a relativism-to-context argument with Frege's (1952) observation that a word has a meaning only in a sentence. It is profitless to discuss the meaning of the word 'saw' in abstraction from such sentences as 'Bring me a saw!', 'Sharpen this saw please', 'You would need a cross cut saw for that job', 'Will this saw do to cut sandstone?', 'Yesterday I saw a double crested mappleworzel', 'I saw the solution in a flash' and so on. Already we seem to be casting a surview over a Wittgensteinian field of family resemblances, if we could rid ourselves of the context of visual perception or logical acuity.

At this point we might be tempted to fall back on the analytical/synthetic distinction, declaring that though there are several homophones in our array of examples they did not carry the same word. The word in which we are interested, 'saw' did have a core meaning, which could be captured in a set of analytical statements, true in every context such as 'a saw is a cutting instrument', 'a saw is an instrument with a serrated cutting edge' and so on, by which the meaning of that word is differentiated from 'hammer' and 'knife'. This line of defence, that there is a universal, stable core of meaning, has been attacked from several directions. We will recruit only those arguments which have been directed to undercutting the stability and exclusiveness of the distinction between analytic and synthetic propositions. Both Quine (1952) and Waismann (1968: ch. 5) argue that where the boundary between these two allegedly radically distinct classes of propositions is drawn, is variable, changing with context, as time goes by and as knowledge develops.

Quine's argument is very simple. Analytic statements differ from other empirical statements only in their content, namely that they report the facts of linguistic usage. These facts are as historically labelled as the facts of demography. There is no set of logically privileged propositions, expressing the universal, core meanings of words.

Waismann's argument goes somewhat deeper. It depends on two ideas. There is the idea of 'open texture' of vocabularies, and the idea of languages as systematically interconnected structures. All languages, even the languages of the most exact sciences, are, so Waismann contended, 'open textured' . By this he meant that the semantic interconnections between linguistic elements are never so completely fixed as to pre-empt all possible uses of these items in all possible future contexts. Thus meaning, even in the most technically sophisticated contexts, is not universal. But at any moment in the development of a science it might be objective, that is based on publicly ascertainable criteria, and it may be foundational, in that there would be locally enforced specifications of a common basis for all meanings in that context at that moment. Take the word 'sodium', a word with a long history in the chemical sciences: at each epoch it has a

range of uses that may seem finally fixed and definitive.
We might choose, say, its specification in chemical terms
by Humphry Davy. The word is to be used for a metal of
a certain specific gravity, isolated from other elements
according to a certain procedure, and when isolated,
having certain well specified dispositions to react with
other substances. For instance it reacts with water, at
room temperatures, yielding hydrogen and sodium hyd-
roxide. The development of the chemical sciences slowly
transformed the semantic specifications of the word. Its
criteria for correct use came to include not only its atomic
weight, but its valency. And its chemical reactivity too
had a role in the way it was classified in the periodic table.
But that place began to take on new meanings as new
criteria, based on subatomic architecture, began to be used
to specify the place of elements in the periodic table.
Through all this turmoil and change the vocable 'sodium'
continued to have a prominent place in the discourse of
scientists.

Since the language of science is open-textured, none of
these moments in the semantic history of the word
'sodium' is a final or definitive moment, the meaning of
the word can shift and change, while it continues to play
its part in the community of chemists, and of other
discursive communities too. But what is this 'word' the
meaning of which can shift? It sounds as if we can
somehow separate the word and its meaning, as if we
could identify the former without the latter.

In his famous series of essays ostensibly on the analytic/
synthetic distinction Waismann drew our attention to
another feature of the historical context-sensitivity of
language use. He gave it no special name, but we could
call it 'systematicity'. As he put it (Waismann, 1968: Ch.
5), referring to the way in which polar pairs of terms came

to be used for degrees of one and the same quality or quantity, 'here we see a whole array of terms shifting in a parallel way.' Though the polar contrast 'hard/soft' is part of the semantic field of the word 'hard', in the physical sciences we have only a scale of hardness, not of softness; we measure the strength of materials, not their weakness. The vocabularies of languages cannot be picked apart into independent components, each with a history of its own independent of the history of others. Historical changes ripple through great stretches of language. Even in the language of the physical sciences there is no semantic core to be found, which could serve as a fixed axis around which historical and cultural variations could be seen to revolve. Yet how can we say that the word 'sodium' has changed its meaning along with other words in the same register, unless there is something stable and invariant, that holds these diverse meanings together into a progression?

It was Wittgenstein who provided the most apt metaphor to resolve the apparent paradox. Fields of meaning are loosely interrelated by similarity or 'family resemblance' relations. Only the vocable is strictly the same from context to context. How is it that some sets of contexts are treated by us as variations of meaning of the same word, while others support more than one word? The 'silly' sheep of the Bible are the blessed ungulates, while the silly sheep of a contemporary hill farm are simply unintelligent animals. Despite historical connections we do not doubt we would agree that it is not the same word, despite its sounding the same. But in the famous Wittgensteinian example of the diversity of what we refer to with the word 'game' we are sure no one would dispute that there is just one word in use in diverse contexts. It is for the latter case that Wittgenstein introduced the image of a 'family resemblance' to express the idea of a structured semantic field. Though there are communalities between each 'adjacent' usage, at the extremities of the field of use there may be nothing in common between what properly count as games.

Therefore the meanings of linguistic expressions (from words to discourses) are functions at some moment of the whole linguistic/cultural system in which they are embedded. We must take account of the open-ended ramifications of interlocking fields of family resemblances. Such a linguistic/cultural system would not be exemplified even by a science, say geology, including its theories, literature, equipment and even jokes. Every expression used in that science owes something to the whole of scientific culture.

This conclusion presupposes another premise: that there is no universal context within which language systems and their coordinated social and material practices would converge. If there were we would, it seems, have given precedence to the Linaean classification of plants over Hopi ethnobotany. This would amount to the concession that even natural kinds are relative to the roles of plants in a culture. The Hopi classification highlights medicinal efficacy, while the Linaean, as currently updated, highlights morphology and lines of descent. There is no way to argue that either has priority in some absolute sense.

Conclusion

Neither the relativist version of Quine's radical translation thesis, nor the absolutist version of Wierzbicka's perfect translation thesis is defensible. The personal and tribal significance of languages in use, which cannot be exhaustively described in terms of the public and/or material circumstances in which the relevant expressions are used, are not inscrutable, but they are not disclosed by the use of a manual of perfect equivalents across languages either. In the work of anthropological psychologists like Lutz (1988) and Much (1995) we can find exemplars of what it takes to make the distinctive personal and tribal meanings of Quine-wise equivalent expressions available to other persons and the members of other tribes. Lutz first assembled a vocabulary of Ifaluk words which seemed to be used in the sorts of situations in which English speakers would use an emotion word, such as farewelling a family member, talking about an occasion on which an important person had been offended, and so on. She then tried to assemble a cluster of English emotion words, each of which referred to an aspect of experience, an experience which was unitary for the Ifaluk. The technique amounts to an extensive development not so much of translation manuals, but of complex linguistic hypotheses about patterns of use. In Much's work the ways various terms for 'possession' by a god are used and the circumstances in which they are appropriate reveal a complex socio-psychological practice, in an account written in English but in which the key words such as *kalasi*, a person possessed or favoured by a god, remain untranslated. As these descriptions spread out from central cases (as presumed from the point of view of the English speaker) the inscrutability of tribal meanings can be systematically dissolved, just as far as one wishes.

A strong variety of semantic relativism would require not only that the meanings of words and other significant signs were functions of cultural complexes, but that these meanings could not be rendered into other languages to become parts of other cultural complexes. While the arguments for semantic relativism support the relativity of

meanings to cultural complexes they do not support a
radical prohibition on some measure of intertranslat-
ability. At best we have a defence of a weak relativism. In
a sense meanings are not universal but it turns out to be
possible to make a fairly convincing case for the possibility
of achieving inter-tribal intelligibility, though this will not
be achieved by construction of translation manuals.

A possible resolution

Perhaps we shall need to acknowledge that there are some
respects in which meanings are local and intelligible only
to people living within a certain cultural-linguistic milieu,
or 'form of life'. But, as Wittgenstein reminds us, we can
construct a hierarchy of forms of life, from the local or
tribal to the universal or human form of life. A form of life
and a language are internally related. The meanings that
characterize a tribal form of life are 'bounded from
within', that is they are peculiar to that form of life and
define it. They are expressed in large measure in the
grammar of the local language. The grammar defines that
form of life. If there were a non-relative semantic theory,
it would have to be based in a universal root vocabulary
internally related to and so definitive of the human form of
life. The human form of life is relatively stable, and
appears in the natural expression of how people feel, what
they want and so on, where these feelings and wants are
close to the biological necessities of life. Thus there is in
principle, a human-kind level bridgehead linking any
language with any other, via the words involved in
linguistic surrogates for natural expressions of those of our
inner states that are most closely involved in the expression of matters of general human biology, such as thirst,
hunger, cold and so on. In the scope of the 'and so on'

there lies the occasion for a good deal of controversy. But wherever the boundary between the universal features of human life and the local features of tribal ways is drawn there is a place in any anthropological science for both the absolute as universal and the relative as local.

NOTES

1 We note in passing Urban's narrative voice, in which, in a sharply defined and distinctive grammatical frame, the first person is used anaphorically. In 'I told her "James said 'I will get the drinks' " ' the embedded 'I' is an anaphor for 'James' (Urban, 1987).
2 We take it that 'charity' means 'the same for all practical purposes'.

3

Epistemic Relativism

Introduction

The topic of this chapter is the claim that knowledge is relative. Much is vague in this formulation. What do we take 'knowledge' to be? What is it supposed to be relative to? And why? We can begin to sharpen up the discussion by settling on the traditional view that knowledge is justified true belief. We would not generally say that someone knew something if they just happened to utter a true statement without any grounds at all. There are two main variants of belief relativism. It may be that what one believes about some topic is different in different circumstances, at different times and differs as one adopts this or that conceptual scheme with which to formulate those beliefs. Or it may be that someone else, usually in different circumstances, holds a different belief about the topic in question. While the topic is in some sense the same, in some way the circumstances affect one's beliefs.

1 *Same person, different belief:* One may at one time believe the members of the government to be trustworthy and at another time, in other circumstances, believe them to be disingenuous.

2 *Different person, different belief.* While I believe the members of the government to be corrupt, someone else, in the same circumstances, may believe ministers to be models of integrity.

For either supposition to make sense as an example of relativism we must assume that the topic is the same for the one believer in both circumstances and for the two believers who differ as to what to believe about it, even in the same circumstances. Perhaps the difference in epistemic attitude of our two believers can be reduced to a case of differences in point of view, both literal and metaphorical, or differences in the historic epoch in which their beliefs were formulated, or the conceptual systems they employed to formulate the beliefs they took to be true. But it may be that people sharing a point of view, an era and a conceptual system or tradition may still differ as to what is properly to be believed concerning some topic. Their beliefs may be relative to their interests which may differ so much as to account for differences in belief.

To the objection that all this can be resolved in favour of absolutism by distinguishing between what people think is knowledge and what really is, the relativist can reply that this distinction is empty. At no time in the past or in the future have we or will we be justified in claiming that we have a body of knowledge which is final, unrevisable and absolute. All we ever have is what we think to be justified true belief. Nor is there any point in proposing an ideal of perfect knowledge, since that ideal is unrealistic and can play no part in our affairs.

We have introduced the topic of epistemic relativism by adopting a traditional view of knowledge, but that view has not gone unchallenged. Since truth seems hard to come by and falsity only ever provisional we mostly make do with something weaker, like 'rationally acceptable and unacceptable beliefs', or something like that. The phrases 'warrantably assertible' and 'not warrantably assertible' are commonly used to express what it is about beliefs that would tempt us to call them 'knowledge'. We have all the evidence we can have for some belief, but though it is not enough to allow us to take the belief to be true, it strongly supports it.

A quite different strategy has been proposed by Popper (1972). In the conception of 'knowledge without a knowing subject' he has introduced the idea of a platonic realm of knowledge items, as a Third World, in which reside such ideal entities as true scientific theories, correct Euclidean proofs and so on. We humans, confined to Worlds One and Two, the worlds of material things and limited human cognition, must make do with conjectures as to what these World Three objects are. It is only our conjectures that can be false. These conjectures are in principle progressively improvable. We test our hypotheses by deducing some of the logical consequences of applying them in specific conditions, and try to find out whether these limited and particular predictions are correct (true) or incorrect (false). If they turn out to be true, all we can rigorously conclude is that the hypothesis under test is so far corroborated, that it has so far not been falsified. But if a prediction turns out to be false we can, *ceteris paribus*, reject the hypothesis upon which it depended. By this means we undertake rigorous attempts to falsify our conjectures about ideal objects such as logically rigorous mathematical proofs, much as we would use the methodology of conjectures and refutations in the investigation of a problem in the physical sciences.

Popper's non-inductive strategy, at least in its starkest form, is open to several serious objections. The ontological status of a realm of beings which are neither material nor discursive is problematic, not least since it seems to be required that it exists prior to our efforts to investigate it. Furthermore it suffers from the general problem of methodological fallibilism, that the supposed asymmetry between confirming a hypothesis as true and disconfirming it as false is difficult to defend. While the former seems to depend on the inductive assumption that the future will be like the past in relevant respects, itself in need of inductive support, the latter seems to depend on a related assumption, that the future will not be unlike the past in relevant respects, an assumption equally in need of inductive support. At the root of the problems that Popper's strategy seems to encounter is a persistence with an ideal of truth, unattainable perhaps but nevertheless operative in defining a rational methodology of enquiry.

Do we escape relativism by dropping the strong demand for truth, a demand which being unachievable tempts us to settle for a conception of knowledge as what we come to hold in the light of a particular and limited method of enquiry? If knowledge is true belief this suggestion seems paradoxical. However, we can reconstruct a weaker form of epistemic relativism using the concept of rational acceptability instead of truth. In some circumstances and in the light of one set of assumptions a certain belief is warrantably assertible, while in other circumstances it is not. It may be that we could be persuaded that the warranted assertibility of beliefs is relative in the ways that relativists have argued that justified true beliefs are properly to be accepted. Since the notion of warranted assertibility is weaker than that of truth, (we could say that a belief was warrantably assertible even though it was not true) the relativity of beliefs of this kind to conceptual resources and historical circumstances is more plausible than a similar claim about the relativity of knowledge.

Protagorean relativism: Truth or warranted assertibility is relative to the person who asserts a proposition

There is a variety of epistemic relativism usually attributed to Protagoras. Plato (1953) presented the doctrine in some detail in the *Theaetetus*, expressed in the famous formula 'Man is the measure of all things'. The first step in the argument is to confine knowledge to what is given by the senses. The relativism of sensory knowledge is obvious: '. . . for instance that which after measurement and comparison we call great, that which after touching we call hot, become respectively small and cold by the presence of greater or hotter objects'. Interestingly Socrates dilutes the relativist force of the argument by claiming that Protagoras never meant to deny that there are wise and unwise people, the former being capable of changing bad beliefs for good ones. This is certainly true when it is a prediction that is called for. Experts are better than laymen.

In our times Protagorean relativism has been taken to mean that a proposition P is true for the person propounding it under the unique circumstances in which he or she propounds it. This means not just that the propounder sincerely believes P, but that P is true relative to the circumstances in which P is propounded. It means, further, that in a different context a different proposition Q may be propounded as true in its unique circumstances. The relativist claim is that considered independently of the persons and their circumstances P and Q may be incompatible. In which case P, propounded in the circumstances of Q, is false. The simplest case of an epistemically relevant variation in circumstances might be that each person has a unique point of view, even just a physical vantage point with which to view the passing scene. I see the duck from my hide and record its colour as blue. You see it from your hide, now with the sun in a different relation to the duck and report it to be green. No duck can be blue and green at once, and the proposition 'The duck is blue', uttered in the circumstances in which it was correct to say 'The duck is green' is false. But according to Protagorean relativism propositions should never be considered independently of the circumstances in which they are propounded and the persons who propound them. This rules out the problematic conclusion we have drawn from the story, since you are forbidden from uttering P in your hide.

The simplest case of a variation among persons that would be epistemically relevant would be when each person has a different way of categorizing what they see before them. One attends to the job people are doing, another to the physiognomy of the workers and so on. I think that a group of aid workers are beautiful in that they sacrifice personal advantage for humanitarian ends, and you think they are ugly because they are gaunt and emaciated as a result of their work in famine devastated areas. We could resolve this problem in just the same way as we resolved the problem of the blue and green duck, by forbidding you to use the word 'beautiful' in your context. A critic might remark that the vocable 'beautiful' is not a bearer of the same word in the two contexts in that the criteria for applying it are so different for you and for me.

Protagorean relativism is an extreme form of truth-relativism. It is extreme in the sense that it makes the truth or warranted assertibility of propositions relative to individual persons on unique occasions. This is a most implausible doctrine, in that we could hardly imagine a coherent form of life developing in such circumstances. But there are other varieties of epistemic relativism which are not so easily dismissed. One could concede the possibility that a very general relativism holds among large scale belief systems without embracing extreme Protagorean individualism.

Evaluative relativism: Truth (warranted assertibility) is relative to the standards by which propositions are evaluated

In the discussion of Protagorean relativism we have assumed that each person employs the same standards as others do in evaluating what they declare to be the case each from his or her own point of view, and with respect to whatever meaning they locally assign to the words and other symbols they are using at different times and on different occasions. However, there is another characterization of relativism more general than that of Protagoras. It could be that each person has more or less the same point of view, or makes allowances for differences in the vantage points of different observers, shares a common system of categories with others, but nevertheless differs from other people with respect to the standards by which they evaluate their beliefs. For instance one person may have set up a very stringent standard for warranting beliefs and another may have settled for a more permissive requirement (Siegel, 1987). If we assume further that there could be no overarching set of evaluative standards by which each person's evaluative standards could be ranked with respect to its knowledge engendering power, then we have a fairly strong form of epistemic relativism. It seems particularly appropriate for topics such as the epistemology of the developing natural sciences and of rival religions. What you take to be a manifestation of God's benevolence I take to be a piece of luck.

An even stronger variety of relativism can be imagined by adding the further condition that along with each set of evaluative standards there is a different set of background beliefs concerning 'the universe, life and everything'. We shall call any such combination of evaluative standards and background beliefs an 'epistemic framework' or simply a 'framework'. Two distinct frameworks may be expressible in the same language and be fully intelligible one from another. It is perfectly possible for someone who evaluates works of art with respect to aesthetic value to understand and even to join in evaluations of those works on the basis of purely monetary considerations. We shall call the body of knowledge that each distinct epistemic framework makes possible a 'knowledge corpus'. According to relativism, there will be many distinct, irreducible knowledge corpora.

Epistemic Frameworks

Fleckian relativism: thought-styles and paradigms

We shall examine arguments arranged around three main ways of conceiving epistemic frameworks. The 'thought-styles' and 'thought-collectives' of Ludwik Fleck ([1921] 1979) are ancestors in modern times of much of the relativism in the interpretation of natural science, usually attributed to T.S. Kuhn (1970). A Fleckian thought-style is not just a way of thinking, but also of carrying on experimental investigations, measurements, assays and so on. Furthermore each thought-style is the way of thinking and acting of a particular group of people, the thought-collective. We must add the qualification 'modern times' to any description of the Fleck/Kuhn idea since the important principle that concepts are intimately involved in the construction of facts and that successive scientific theories are dominated by leading ideas was expounded in detail by William Whewell in the nineteenth century. According to Whewell there are a number of epistemological antitheses evident in the development of the natural sciences. They can be lined up in mutually interrelated pairs. Whewell lists 'thoughts and things', 'necessary and experiential truths' and 'theories and facts' among others. Each pair defines a progressive interaction so that what we take to be the facts is influenced by the theories we hold, and in their turn these theories are influenced by the development of our knowledge of facts (Whewell, 1847: Ch. II). Just such a theory/fact interrelation is a central feature of the relation between Fleckian thought-styles and the bodies of knowledge that they make possible. We shall discuss this connection of a framework in terms of the agenda set by Kuhn, namely with frameworks defined in Kuhn's way as paradigms.

Another way of analysing epistemic frameworks can be found in the writings of Collingwood (1940). He provides a powerful account of the structure and hierarchical organization of a knowledge engendering framework. Collingwood's conception of an intellectual enterprise is based on the idea of a sequence or interlinked sequences of questions and answers. Each question/answer pair presupposes the answer to another deeper question. Each question/answer sequence rests on a bedrock of absolute presuppositions. These presuppositions do not arise correlated from a corresponding set of questions.

Finally we turn to an alternative formulation to both the above, to the idea of 'framework' as narrative, an idea somewhat deliberately set askew to that of the paradigm. This is the idea of epistemic judgements developing over time, in relation to a tradition. This more dynamic conception of framework has been advocated in various ways by other authors, for example Stephen Toulmin.

According to Toulmin (1961) the scientist '*begins* with the conviction that . . . some fixed set of laws or patterns or mechanisms accounts for Nature's following the course it does, and that his understanding of these should guide his expectations'. A sequence of different 'ideals of natural order' can be seen at work in shaping the expectations and ways of theorizing of the scientists of the seventeenth century. But like Collingwood's absolute presuppositions, ideals of natural order are not arrived at inductively nor are they abandoned because they have been shown to be false by experiment or observation.

The argument from multiple paradigms

The popular version of this argument is derived from the writings of Thomas Kuhn. Kuhn's argument for a 'relativist' interpretation of the natural sciences involves three main points:

1 Paradigm change transforms the science in which it occurs by transforming the standards governing what are to count as acceptable solutions to problems.
2 The post-paradigm normal science tradition that emerges from a paradigm change is 'not only incompatible but also incommensurable with that which has gone before' (Kuhn, 1970).

3　Since the perceptual gestalten through which scientists
　　perceive the world are changed when paradigms
　　change the post-paradigm world-as-perceived will be
　　different from the pre-paradigm world (Kuhn, 1970).

Not only does a paradigm switch alter an inquirer's
explanatory scheme in some rather dramatic ways but it
also changes what that person thinks the explanatory
scheme is offered to explain. There is at once an epistemological and an ontological switch. Theories offered in
different paradigms are simply 'about' different things.
Joseph Priestley interpreted his experiments in terms of
'phlogiston', the matter of fire, and so discovered 'dephlogistated air'. Lavoisier interpreted his experiments in
terms only of 'positive' substances, and so he discovered
'oxygen'. But the 'things' referred to by theories couched
in different paradigms are not wholly different, at least
according to Kuhn. In this case we can say that the same
stuff was 'dephlogistated air' for Priestley and 'oxygen' for
Lavoisier. Interparadigmatic translation can be effected
given sufficient time, effort, and patience. Kuhn offers
certain trans-paradigmatic conditions which can be relevantly brought into discussion of justifications for paradigm switches. These include relative puzzle solving
ability, explanatory power, predictive power, neatness,
suitability, and simplicity. The Priestley/Lavoisier example shows that for paradigm connections and comparisons
to be possible, at least in some cases, a generic ontology
must be shared by all three parties, the adherents to the
paradigms and we who strive to forge the connection. 'I
do not believe that it [the communication breakdown] is
ever total or beyond recourse. Where he [P.K. Feyera-
bend] talks of incommensurability *tout court*, I have regu-
larly spoken . . . of partial communication, and I believe it

can be improved upon to whatever extent circumstances may demand and patience permit . . .' (Kuhn, 1970: 7).

If paradigm shifts necessitated complete shifts in subject matter there would be no possibility of hunting for the grounds for rational choice among paradigms. Paradigm shifts, within the framework of that Western scientific tradition which had its origins in the ancient Greek traditions of enquiry, have never involved root and branch transformations of generic ontologies. The deep, generic ontology of individual substances and their attributes, located in the manifolds of space and time, has persisted however radically versions of this ontology have differed one from another. Incommensurability between paradigms has never been so radical and deep that it has not been possible to recognize this generic ontology embedded in every successive world view, even in contemporary field theories.

Commentary

Meaning and incommensurability   There has been a persistent tendency to recruit Kuhn to the ranks of those who, like Goodman (1978), hold that different frameworks engender different worlds. However we believe that in doing so Kuhn's views have been misunderstood. One of the main sources of misunderstanding derives from his unfortunate use of the word 'incommensurability'. According to Kuhn, two theories are incommensurable if there is no common fact of the matter by which a decision as to which of the theories was the more worthy of belief could be rationally based; that is their belief worthiness cannot be subjected to a common 'measure'. Typically, theories are said to be incommensurable if they are drawn from different and rival paradigms. Kuhn seems to suggest that paradigm shifts necessitate meaning shifts, but it is not clear that meaning shifts must lead to mutually incommensurable theories, nor incommensurability in the above sense to a radical break in meaning, to the extent that mutual intelligibility is lost. If we took incommensurability in its strong or radical form in which it is linked with radical disparities in meanings, we would have to say that demonstrations that the mass of a moving body is greater than the mass of that body at rest in some frame of reference could not be used to refute Newtonian theory, because the concept of 'mass' in Special Relativity is not the same as the concept of 'mass' in classical physics. Yet it is clear that the scientific community did think that the experimental results of certain studies of pi-mesons showed that $m = m_0 \sqrt{1 - v^2/c^2}$ is to be preferred to $m = m_0$. We have seen in chapter 2 there are no really knock-down arguments for absolute untranslatability of terminology between any pair of *human* languages, let alone between the dialects of scientific communities in the Western scientific tradition! History favours a weaker reading of Kuhn's thesis of incommensurability, a reading according to which incommensurability does not entail that there is an unbridgeable semantic gulf. Kuhn nowhere shows that meaning shifts are necessitated by paradigm shifts. His historical examples support only the weaker thesis that limited meaning shifts have occurred as paradigms have been replaced or transformed.

Let us look more closely at the relation between paradigms and meanings. An argument to link them internally might run something like this: every concept in a scientific paradigm is tied to the prevailing ontology, for example 'Heat is a molecular motion'. If the ontology of physics changes in such a way that 'molecule' is no longer a meaningful term in our theoretical vocabulary, say because we have opted for continuous fluids as the basic physical beings, and that sort of change is the core of a paradigm shift, 'heat' can no longer be defined by the use of the term. The meaning of the expression 'heat' and all those that are semantically related to it such as 'temperature', 'calorific value', and so on must also change in such a way that the meaningfulness of the term 'molecule' is not presupposed in our understanding of any of them.

However there is another interpretation of this little piece of fictional history. Suppose we could recreate the meaning of 'molecule' in our new vocabulary, say as an imaginary device, a discrete element of a fluid. We have set up the concept of 'molecule' in the new ontology, that is the term is now once again meaningful. But, in this ontology it is plain that there are no molecules. Statements about molecules in the context of a continuous fluids ontology, are like statements about unicorns in the context of an ontology of horses, cows and pigs. We can say meaningfully that unicorns have silver hooves, manes of purest white and so on. But there aren't any! If translatability between meanings of concepts under two paradigms can be effected in this sort of way then should we be speaking of two paradigms? Certainly the vocable 'heat' does not mean the same thing in the two frameworks. It is a state of strain in a continuous medium in the one and a molecular motion in the other. Yet the term 'molecule' is meaningful in both paradigms, though the meanings differ. What should we say? We might say that theories in different paradigms are incommensurable because there is no set of common terms with the same meaning in each paradigm. The only thing linking the two is the shape or sound of the vocable 'molecule'. Or should we say that there are common terms, such as 'molecule', but that they were thought to pick out something real by those who subscribed to one paradigm and are not thought to do so by subscribers to the other? There seems to be no clear resolution of this conundrum. This seems to us to reflect the vagueness of the Kuhnian notion of 'paradigm' and the difficulty we have in trying to give it a useful application in concrete cases, fictional or otherwise. The underlying problem is the vagueness of the import of 'same word'.

Different paradigms, different worlds?   How are we to make sense of the idea that paradigm shifts engender 'different worlds'? The idea is not at all puzzling if it is simply the claim that a paradigm shift permits different aspects or features of the world to be attended to, recognized, classified, studied and so on, from the aspects which were the focus of attention before. Proponents of two paradigms might well engage in meaningful discourse about distinct subject matters. For a neo-Platonist the important thing about metals was their colours. The dull grey of lead spoke eloquently of its relation to Saturn, the bright red of copper of its relation to Mars. For an atomic physicist the important thing to pay attention to is the relative atomic weights of the metals, as revealed by the use of Aston's mass spectrograph. It seems to us that when a neo-Platonist and an atomic physicist discuss such matters as the cost of flashing for a roof, or the best way to fix sheathing on the hull of a boat, they are talking about and dwelling in the very same world. They can happily discuss the merits and properties of copper, iron and so on, whatever they may believe about the real natures of these substances. Different aspects of the world are available to human observers and experimenters as they adopt this or that paradigm. But the claim that in the course of a paradigm change someone comes to inhabit a different world we can only regard as a piece of over-dramatic rhetoric. The shared patterns of everyday experience persist while conceptions of the underlying structures of material things provided by the sciences may change radically.

Are standards of evaluation of claims to knowledge relative to paradigms? Does a change of paradigm necessitate a change in standards of evaluation? Whether we believe that the distinctive properties of metals arise from differences in the balance of the Hot, the Cold, the Wet and the Dry, as was thought at one time, or from different distributions of protons, neutrons and electrons as we now believe, no necessary equivocation of evaluative concepts seems to be entailed. While Aston classifies metals by their atomic weights, his neo-Platonist friend classifies them by their colours. However it seems to us that the standards of careful watchfulness, of being on guard against self-deception, of the use of Mill's methods in the evaluation of evidence, and so on, may *and should* be employed by both. Differences there may be in where authority is held to lie. But both share the idea that knowledge is not a matter of whim or ungrounded intuition.

How should we classify Kuhn's 'relativism' in the framework of our three fold scheme? Kuhn is some sort of relativist in so far as he detaches his point of view from many absolutist assumptions. The tie between paradigm shift and gestalt switch would serve to delete any strong foundationalist flavour from philosophy of science, yet the idea of 'gestalt switch' is more a metaphor for a change of interpretations of what we see and hear than a psychological theory of perception for Kuhn. How things look, feel, taste and smell serve as reference points in any epistemology of the natural sciences. But to the extent that he allows cross-paradigm intelligibility he must allow a measure of scientific progress. Furthermore if we adopt the commonsense way of understanding what could be meant by paradigm changes leading to 'different worlds', as the making salient of different aspects of the world, we gain in intelligibility what we lost in drama! Kuhn's relativism is mildly anti-foundationalist in that different groups of investigators are likely to take different aspects of the world as salient for their studies. However we are unable to see that Kuhn's historiography of paradigms is anti-universalist in its implications. Nothing in Kuhn's account entails that in the end one paradigm may not come to serve as the settled basis for all further scientific studies. Though, of course, nothing in the history of science can say that it will. At the same time the establishment of a common, unified scientific world-view could not be universalist in the sense of demanding hegemony over all other ways of construing human experience, not least because of the ubiquitous role of values in actual lives.

But is it anti-objectivist? In one sense it is. Kuhn's position is perspectivalist in that different aspects of the world are available to different people from different cultures with different conceptual systems and different apparatus and interests in using it. This is a weak anti-objectivism, a benign relativism as we have defined that notion in chapter 1. If every paradigm brings out some aspect of the world, however partial and minor, in a sense every paradigm contributes to human knowledge.

Absolute presuppositions and question/answer hierarchies

According to R.G. Collingwood's theory of absolute presuppositions (Collingwood, 1940), systematic inquiries should be understood as a series of related claims the presuppositions of which give rise to questions, to which these claims are answers. Whether certain responses are legitimate answers (rather than true ones) depends upon their sharing the presuppositions of the questions to which they are meant to be answers. At the base of the series of questions and answers are *absolute presuppositions* which are not answers to any questions at all – or at least questions that properly speaking appear within the systematic enquiry then being pursued. They are given and are the most basic presuppositions of that systematic enquiry. So, the term 'absolute' should not be understood in an absolute sense. It should be understood as absolute *relative* to the enquiry to which it is absolute. According to Collingwood, within the systematic enquiry in question, it makes no sense to ask if the absolute presupposition is true or false. Even to ask such a question implies that one has the option of rejecting the absolute presupposition if confronted with compelling argument or evidence to the contrary. But these presuppositions are not open to that sort of critical review, unless one is prepared to cease regarding the given presupposition as absolute. But that would be to step outside the systematic enquiry in question. So, whether questions of truth or justification are appropriate depends upon the place of a presupposition in a given systematic inquiry.

In this way Collingwood's absolute presuppositions are very similar to Wittgenstein's boundary propositions. Since the negation of a boundary proposition is meaningless, such propositions are neither true nor false. They express the grammar of the discourses that sustain a form of life. Since *relative presuppositions* are presuppositions which answer prior questions they must have a truth value with respect to the context defined by the absolute presup-

positions of the inquiry in hand. But the logical efficacy of
a presupposition – its power to give rise to a question –
does not depend upon the truth or falsity of the presupposition. Thus *absolute presuppositions* are logically efficacious
but lack truth value. There are no prior questions to which
they are answers.

Collingwood (1940: ch. 5) holds that the meaning of a
particular question or answer is a function of the meaning
of its presupposition(s). And the meaning of such a
presupposition(s) is a function, in turn, of its presupposi-
tion(s). Ultimately, the meaning of a particular question
or answer is a function of the meaning of the absolute
presupposition(s) of the inquiry in which those questions
or answers appear. 'The answer to any question presupposes whatever the question presupposes' (Collingwood, 1940: 63). A questioner or respondent for
whom the question is appropriate, that is, for whom the
question arises, is committed to supposing the presupposi-
tion(s) of the question.

Since, for Collingwood, relative presuppositions have
truth-value and absolute presuppositions have not,
questions of verification and truth can be asked intelligibly
only about relative presuppositions. To pose questions
about verification or truth of absolute presuppositions is to
engage in what Collingwood calls 'pseudo-metaphysics'
(Collingwood, 1940: 162–3). Whereas questions of verification and truth of relative presuppositions admit of
alternative answers, questions of verification and truth of
absolute presuppositions do not (Collingwood, 1940: 37–
40; 1940: 31–2). Absolute presuppositions are culturally
inherited and not acquired through argument or from
evidence.

There are systematic shifts of meaning of key concepts
between different enquiries, simply because absolute pre-

suppositions determine such meanings. Though there might appear to be the same terms in different sets of absolute presuppositions that define different enquiries, the meanings of those terms must differ. Such differences constitute, in part, the distinctness of different systematic enquiries. The meaning and the truth of a proposition depend upon the question which the proposition answers, and therefore cannot be known without recourse to the question which the proposition answers (Collingwood, 1940: 30, 33). Whether two presuppositions mean the same thing depends upon their both answering the same question. No relative presupposition in one systematic enquiry could mean the same as one in another enquiry, nor could it mean the same thing as the same form of words serving in another enquiry as an absolute presupposition. For example the principle of the conservation of energy was a relative presupposition in scientific enquiries in Kant's time, since it was an 'assistant' to the principle of conservation of matter. In the nineteenth century the principle of conservation of energy superseded the principle of conservation of matter as an absolute presupposition (Collingwood, 1940: 264–8).

One cannot be aware of one's own absolute presuppositions. 'If people became aware that in certain contexts they were in the habit of treating this or that presupposition as an absolute one, they would be unable to go on doing it'. (1940: 96). So, according to Collingwood, the metaphysician's job is historical. It is to uncover the absolute presuppositions of previous thinkers. A metaphysical claim should be read as introduced by the 'metaphysical rubric,' namely, 'so and so absolutely presupposed such and such'. A 'metaphysical' statement not introduced by this rubric is a piece of 'pseudo-metaphysics'.

Commentary

Just how relativist is Collingwood's theory of knowledge? Could several Collingwoodian question/answer hierarchies be synthesized into one unified system? Only if each set of absolute presuppositions were incompatible would there be a principled way of denying that sets of absolute presuppositions could be conjoined into new and larger sets, thus unifying the question/answer hierarchies. But since absolute presuppositions do not have truth-values the relation of incompatibility between epistemic frameworks cannot be characterized as any kind of contradiction or contrariety. We cannot say that if one set is true all the others are false, or that no two sets can be true together. These assessments simply do not apply. Collingwood's solution to the question of how to distinguish knowledge engendering procedures by reference to sets of absolute presuppositions is to suggest that incompatible absolute presuppositions are 'non-consupponible'. But this means only that they cannot be supposed together. It does not explain why that is so.

Collingwood's scheme is mildly anti-foundationalist in the sense that while each pattern of enquiry is strongly founded on its set of absolute presuppositions, there is no common foundation for all patterns of enquiry, provided we accept the unanalysed notion of the non-consupponibility of distinct sets of absolute presuppositions. Accepting that principle is tantamount to accepting the principle that no common set of absolute presuppositions, forming a foundation for all inquiries, could be created.

Is it anti-objectivist? There is nothing in Collingwood's argument to suggest that absolute presuppositions may not be objective, in the sense of independent of anyone's point of view. However, sharing a point of view as to the objective nature of the world may still find us choosing different sets of absolute presuppositions. Choice of absolute presuppositions, Collingwood emphasizes, does not depend on any prior beliefs. Even where we share a great deal there may simply be prejudice that explains our differences. We are both Christians, holding it to be objectively true that Christ was the Son of God, but you believe in papal infallibility as an absolute presupposition of your Christian faith while I do not. But Collingwood's position on the consupponibility of sets of absolute presuppositions is certainly compatible with a rejection of any common ground which is taken to be objective by those working within different sets of absolute presuppositions.

Is it anti-universalist? Even if we assume that there is a common world to which all enquiries are directed each pattern of enquiry would reveal only aspects of that world, of what really happened and so on. Given again that sets of absolute presuppositions are not consupponible no single question/answer hierarchy could be synthesized from the collection of historically given multitudes of such hierarchies, which would bring to light every possible aspect of the world that we might come to know. No pattern of enquiry could reveal the whole world. This is the anti-universalist consequence to which Collingwood's arguments and analyses point.

The argument from distinctive traditions

The third source of epistemic relativism that we identified at the beginning of this chapter was based on the idea of distinctive knowledge traditions. According to this point of view it is only retrospectively that a series of theories can be appraised. In other words, what is appraised is always a history. It is not just a series of epistemically independent and atomic theories which is appraised one by one. It is a whole series or tradition the members of which stand in various complex relationships to each other through time which is appraised. Indeed, what we take to be a single theory is always 'a growing developing entity, one which cannot be considered a static structure . . . . To evaluate a theory, just as to evaluate a series of theories . . . is precisely to write that history, that narrative of defeats and victories' (MacIntyre, 1977: 468–69). According to us, there is no such thing as an isolated theory, only a moment in the development of a theory-family (Harré, 1983: ch. 4).

Among the marks of a successful theory is that it enables us to understand its predecessors in a newly intelligible way. At one and the same time, it enables us to understand precisely why its predecessors have had to be rejected or modified and also why, without and before its illumination, past theory could have seemed credible. It introduces new standards for evaluating the past. It recasts the narrative which constitutes the continuous reconstruction of the scientific tradition. 'Scientific reason turns out to be subordinate to, and intelligible only in terms of historical reason' (MacIntyre, 1977: 467).

The idea that we must regard scientific theories, and indeed works of art as well, as growing and developing entities and not static structures, suggests that the appraisal of these cultural entities must be historical. Making them intelligible requires the construction of a narrative. For MacIntyre, all that needs to be said about progress and evaluation is to be found within the history of pertinent theorizing itself. There is no need, indeed no possibility, of appealing to some realm independent of such historicizing. There are no narrative independent foundations by reference to which theories (or other cultural entities including works of art) could be appraised absolutely.

Commentary

An argument for this view can be constructed by reflecting on the idea of 'past actuality', or what it is to hold to some historical 'fact of the matter'.

> Events (or more precisely, descriptions of events) are not the raw material out of which narratives are constructed; rather an event is an abstraction from a narrative. An event may take five seconds or five months, but in either case whether it is one event or many depends upon not a definition of 'event' but on a particular narrative construction which generates the event's appropriate description. This concept of 'event' is not remote from our ordinary responses to stories; in certain stories we can accept even something like the French Revolution as a simple event, because that is the way it is related to characters and plot, while in other stories it may be too complex to describe as a single whole. But if we accept that the description of events is a function of particular narrative structures, we cannot at the same time suppose that the actuality of the past is an untold story. There can in fact be no untold stories at all, just as there can be no unknown knowledge. There can be only past facts not yet described in a context of narrative form (Mink: 1978: 147).

We have quoted this passage at length because it illustrates with remarkable clarity the kind of slide from epistemology to ontology that weakens so much relativist argument. Mink is right to remind us that what is to count as a fact is relative to whatever narrative we are currently constructing. So what events we pick out, put together, rearrange and so on in the process of telling the tale are what the historian of France (or the atomic theory) has to work with. But that does not entail that the French past or the architecture of atoms is merely a narrative construction. There was The Terror and there are protons, neutrons and electrons arranged in different ways. To slip into relativism here is to commit what Bhaskar (1975: 16) has called the 'epistemic fallacy'. To try to force the work of historians into either a realist or a constructionist epistemology is to do violence to the subtle way that different points of view display different aspects of what there is or has been. There is no point of view from which 'reality as a whole' is visible.

Interestingly Mink adds a coherentist account of 'resilience' in historical narratives, by appeal to the degree of coherent consensus amongst interlocking narratives, each championed by a suitably qualified practitioner. The construction of history, therefore, is not arbitrary. Just as we have seen with each epistemic relativism that we have encountered, the fact that different aspects of the world become available to us from different points of view, quite fails to support the kind of radical conclusion that thrills the reader of the more extravagant post-structuralist and post-modernist works. As Mink himself says, 'historical narratives are capable of displacing each other. . . . when a narrative makes sense of a series of actions by showing them to be decisions reflecting a consistently held policy, where received accounts could only describe them as arbitrary and surprising reactions, or as irrational responses' (Mink, 1978: 152).

When a narrative seems to face the story of a recalcitrant episode it would seem that for the narrativist two options are always open; viz., reconceptualize the episode to fit the unfolding narrative or change the narrative to fit the best account we have of the episode. The Shakespearean narrative in which Richard III plays the role of villain is challenged by an alternative story of what happened to the Princes in the Tower. In the absence of any principled way of deciding which strategy to adopt a strongly construct-ivist version of the narrativist approach would be too weak to vindicate its claim to be the prime way of producing a corpus of historical knowledge. The same problem arises in traditional philosophy of science, since it seems that any experimental results can be rejigged to fit any theory. Yet in practice many stories of experiments prove recalcitrant. There are limits to permissible 'fixing'!

In practice historians, scientists and all other persons who are certified by their apprenticeship to a tradition of knowledge production as the tellers of tales adopt a simple principle: no single recalcitrant episode may unseat a narrative. *Narratives unseat narratives*. Every description of an episode occurs within a narrative context. So when examining the strain between a recalcitrant episode and an unfolding narrative we must examine that episode's encapsulated narrative along with the unfolding narrative. The recalcitrant episode may be shelved until the unfold-ing narrative becomes sufficiently rich to incorporate the episode in reconceptualized form, or the story of the episode is retold, or if there are enough other such recalcitrant episodes which, taken together, threaten the line of the unfolding narrative it may be transformed to accommodate them. In this way paradigm shifts absorb anomalies. When that happens alternative competing nar-ratives are compared and judged according to such values as accuracy, consistency, scope, simplicity, fruitfulness, comprehensiveness, cogency, openness to further narrat-izing, or the like. And these meta-theoretical values are nonfoundationally articulable within the terms of the historian-critic's own historic place.

Once again we find a relativism that is anti-foundationalist yet not incompatible with the idea that a universal story might in the end be told. However in the quotation from Mink we can see a slide into an unwarranted anti-objectivism, at least by the arguments he sketches. Nothing he offers goes any way to showing that the narrative relative 'facts' that historians, scientists and so on come up with are not genuine aspects of an independent reality. Of course that negative observation does not establish that they are. The fact that episodes enter into larger narratives only as stories no more shores up an anti-universalist and anti-objectivist line than does the perspectivity we encountered in the writings of Kuhn and Collingwood. The matter is more subtle. Each thought-style and each independent enquiry resting on its absolute presuppositions, each paradigm and each tradition reveal different aspects of the world. No one of these frameworks reveals every aspect of the world as it is. But these observations support only a benign relativism. The use of each framework has something to contribute to our knowledge of the nature of the world and of human history.

A Global Argument Against Epistemic Relativism

The arguments for various levels and kinds of epistemic relativism, that we have discussed in this chapter, have depended on the idea that there are independent and irreducible thought-styles, sets of absolute presuppositions, paradigms, narrative conventions and so on. In general these could be subsumed under one very general idea, that of the 'conceptual scheme' (Harré, 1963). Donald Davidson (1984) argued that relativism is not coherently formulable, since it requires the idea of a conceptual scheme and that idea, so he claims to show, is incoherent. Without that idea we cannot entertain the possibility of multiple and irreducible conceptual schemes. In his account, the idea of a conceptual scheme is incoherent because it requires that there be some other, independent but coexisting, conceptual scheme in contrast to which the former can be discerned as different and distinct. If there were a truly distinctive conceptual scheme it could not, declares Davidson, be translated into the contrasting scheme so that it could be discerned to be different and distinct. Davidson's argument has the form of a dilemma. To make sense of the possibility of a putatively alternative conceptual scheme we would have to know that such a scheme existed. But to know this we would have to have achieved the translation of at least some items from that scheme into our current one, to realize that they were not the same as any of ours. But if that had been achieved the putative alternative would not be a genuine alternative conceptual scheme because translation would have been effected into our scheme and so the two would have become one. If we could distinguish one conceptual scheme from another we should need to know what the other comprised, but if we did know this it would be a part of our conceptual scheme or could be rendered as part of it by translation, so it would not be an alternative conceptual scheme. Failing our ability to distinguish our conceptual scheme from an alternative conceptual scheme the notion of a conceptual scheme is incoherent. The idea of a conceptual scheme is incoherent because the idea of an alternative conceptual scheme is incoherent. Thus relativism – which requires the idea of more than one mutually irreducible conceptual scheme – is incoherent too.

However, the weakness of this argument is obvious. As MacIntyre (1989) and others have remarked, we need not define the otherness of a conceptual scheme in terms of its untranslatability into some terms of our conceptual scheme. Linguistic anthropologists are very familiar with the phenomenon of understandability without translatability. We can understand an alien conceptual scheme, say the emotionology of the Ifaluk (Lutz, 1988) by assembling rough verbal correspondences and embedding the untranslatable terms in a large repertoire of anecdotes which illustrates their use. People do speak more than one language, and we don't say that by learning other languages they are expanding their first language. If the argument does not hold for languages it certainly does not hold for conceptual schemes.

The Paradoxes of Epistemic Relativism

Starting with our original formulation of epistemic relativism, the Protagorean form, we can construct a paradox. The very claim that a belief may be true for one person and false for another is itself a belief that is supposed to be true for all. If that is so, then there is at least one belief that is not relative in the Protagorean sense, so strong Protagorean relativism is false if it is true. This paradox has been described by Maurice Mandelbaum (1982), Harvey Siegel (1987) and others. Understood as relativism of truth, Protagorean relativism denies 'the existence of any standard or criterion higher than the [assessments or values of an] individual by which claims to truth and knowledge can be adjudicated' (Siegel, 1987: 4). Looking deeper into the paradoxical nature of Protagorean relativism we could argue against it on the grounds that it 'undermines the very notion of rightness', as Siegel puts it. If anything can be true in virtue of one's believing it to be so, then it could be false in virtue of someone else's believing it so. How could we then commend or reject the beliefs of others? If all force to the distinction between right and wrong is leached out what can be made of the implicit claim by those who write in favour of relativism that it is the right, the best or the most reasonable epistemic doctrine to adopt?

Looking at the other side of the argument of the first section of this chapter we might conclude instead that Protagorean relativism entailed that every belief was true in that it is possible that somewhere and at some time someone will have believed it. By the same token it is just as likely that someone else will have disbelieved it. If all it takes for a belief to be false is that someone disbelieves it then there will be many beliefs which are both true and false. If we all continue to adhere to the principle of non-contradiction it seems that the only possible conclusion to draw is that there can be no general truths and no general falsehoods. But Protagorean relativism purports to be just such a general truth. Therefore if it is true it is incoherent.

However this argument is seriously flawed as an attack on the Protagorean position. It holds only if we have, in a sense, already abandoned Protagoreanism. The very meaning of truth on the Protagorean view is equivocal as between two people, one of whom affirms P as true and the other affirms not-P as true. There is no genuine contradiction to be resolved. The very doctrine of Protagorean relativism may be held to be true by some and not by others. This would not lead to contradictions. The

worst that would obtain would be a kind of incommensurability or cross-purposeness. The upshot of this would
be not that relativism entails, self-refutingly, that there are
global contradictions between the philosophical theses
people believe and the practices in which they engage on
the basis of their belief in them. Rather where Protagorean
relativism obtains there could be no such contradictions. A
Protagorean relativist is not obliged to hold that all beliefs
and opinions are true. Epistemic attitudes are individual-
ized to persons. A Protagorean relativist might hold that
the earth is a sphere and that it is false that it is a circular
plate, at the same time being well aware that someone else
holds that it is flat. To each the other displays 'invincible
ignorance' *and there is nothing to be done about it.* The fact
that somewhere over the rainbow someone else is probably affirming what one denies, or denying what one
affirms is neither here nor there to a Protagorean relativist.

Protagorean relativism is a relativism with respect to
truth or falsity taken as a bipolar or bivalent opposition.
Only in that respect does it run the risk of collapsing into
solipsism. While it denies a standard of truth above and
beyond the epistemic values of the person to whom
something seems true, it leaves open the possibility that
there are other epistemic values, with respect to which
Protagorean relativisms may not be so obviously defective. Rightness, reasonableness, appropriateness, aptness,
etc. may well have standards that go beyond the stringen-
cies of bivalent truth and falsity, and that may obtain
across more than one conceptual scheme, thought-style,
set of narrative conventions and so on. We shall look at
this alternative in discussing the views of Margolis (1980)
in chapter 7.

Fleckian relativism, however, comes from the realization that the source of potential variability in what is taken

to be knowledge is not the individual person, but rather is to be found in intercommunal differences realized in all sorts of knowledge garnering practices. It is the thought-collective to which a thought-style belongs, and each individual partakes of that thought-style in so far as they are each a member of a certain thought-collective. For the most careful working out of an epistemic relativism informed by the distinction we have just drawn between Protagorean and Fleckian relativism we must consult the Strong Programme now associated with the names of Barry Barnes (1977) and David Bloor (1976).

The Strong Programme: Is it a Sociological Reduction?

What can vary, collective to collective? In different cultures and in different epochs, different conceptual systems are readily discerned in the discourses of members. Where one will treat probability as a relative frequency another will treat it as a representation of strength of belief. The word is the same but the concept is very different. Where one will explain combustion by reference to gains and losses of phlogiston another will use the concept of oxygen as the basis of explanations. The phenomena are the same but the explanations are different. There may also be differences between the criteria for assessing beliefs used in different thought-collectives. Some may be content with coherence with an existing body of knowledge as a reason for belief, while others will want a point by point comparison with what counts in their circle as the facts of the matter.

What can vary person to person? Certainly there are variations between persons in the conceptual systems that they use and also in the criteria by which they assess claims to knowledge. According to Fleck this kind of inter-personal difference comes from adherence to or member-ship in different thought-collectives. But more central to the genesis of the Strong Programme, according to Man-icas and Rosenberg (1985) is interpersonal variance in the very phenomena of experience. Two people, placed in similar situations, as these would be judged by a third party, may differ in what they experience. There may be no way by which such differences could be expressed. We may successfully communicate about our experience with-out our having exactly the same experiences, that is qualitatively the same. For example we can use colour words for interpersonal communication about all sorts of matters, including matching of fabrics, criticism of paint-ings and so on, though we know that the qualia or simple colour sensations each of us experiences are logically incomparable.

The Strong Programme aims at filling the gap between the paucity of what one might call the 'official evidence' on which knowledge claims are alleged to be based and the strength of conviction with which such beliefs are held in this or that thought-collective. At the same time it aims at excising the radical scepticism which would follow from a radical individualizing of the process of knowledge gar-nering and the radical personalizing of conceptual resources. Relativism would then be defined by the idea that the grounds for belief are culture relative so what is known is relative to thought-collective and thought-style. This does not, as we shall show, entail the abandonment of the idea that the natural sciences treat of a world independent of human thoughts and wishes.

The Strong Programme can be defined by four tenets (Bloor, 1976). These are

1 *The tenet of causality*: [The inquiry] would be causal, that is, concerned with the conditions which bring about belief or states of knowledge. Naturally there will be other types of causes apart from social ones which will cooperate in bringing about belief.

2 *The tenet of impartiality*: It [the Strong Programme] would be impartial with respect to truth and falsity, rationality and irrationality, success or failure. Both sides of these dichotomies would require explanation.

3 *The tenet of symmetry*: It would be symmetrical in its style of explanation. The same types of causes would explain, say, true and false beliefs.

4 *The tenet of reflexivity*: It would be reflexive. In principle its patterns of explanation would have to be applicable to sociology itself.

At least as thus defined the Strong Programme does not seem to be concerned with the origins of the conceptual systems that are involved in the genesis and assessment of putative facts.

The Strong Programme cannot be understood properly without the explicit addition of two crucial features, both involving a kind of residual realism. In their admirable exposition of the Strong Programme Manicas and Rosenberg (1988: 53) distinguish between 'single barrelled' and 'double barrelled' realism. There is a modest view shared by many realists (Harré, 1986), that the world-as-it-is plays an indispensable role in the genesis of knowledge though we only ever encounter limited aspects of it. Then there is the very much stronger view, that the world as it is can be fully known, and is that to which true propositions correspond. In the former view the world is only a part-cause of our veridical experience, while in the latter it is the whole cause of that which we experience veridically.

The single-barrelled realism of the Strong Programme depends on the thesis that the world is not experienced as it is in itself, but only in its effects on us. Those effects are always 'mediated by socially constituted forms' (Manicas and Rosenberg, 1988: 56). Barnes (1977: 25) puts the matter plainly: '. . . this reality should not be identified with any linguistic account of it, or, needless to say, with any way of perceiving it, or pictorial representation of it. Reality is the source of our primitive causes, which, having been reprocessed by our perceptual apparatus, produce changes in our knowledge and the verbal representations of it which we possess.'

If we combine these addenda with the rejection of epistemic individualism, the idea that knowledge is something possessed only by individuals, we come to an account of how a common body of knowledge or belief is possible. It is not common experience that unites a scientific community since, according to Barnes and Bloor, there is and can be no such thing. But it is the possibility of communication, that comes from the possession of a common language. This possession is understood in the manner of the later Wittgenstein. Presumably, in so far as languages differ, the mediated common stock of beliefs they make possible will also differ. But according to single-barrelled realists the world constrains what it is possible to experience by the use of any collectively mediated linguistic and practical cultural system, say that of physics.

In 1977 Barnes drew a relativist conclusion from his qualified realism. It is this conclusion perhaps that has led many critics to attack the Strong Programme as more relativist than it was ever intended to be. Barnes wrote (1977: 25) 'That the structure of our verbal knowledge does not thereby necessarily converge upon a single form isomorphous with what is real, should not surprise us. Why ever should we expect this to be a property of our linguistic and cognitive capabilities?' The weaknesses in this brief argument are only too obvious. To know that our knowledge does or does not conform necessarily or contingently to the structure of reality we would need to know the form of the real already. It is also entirely obvious why we should expect some convergence between knowledge and reality. By the use of knowledge acquired in a disciplined enquiry we do manage rather well in this world. We would expect there to be a convergence and are greatly surprised when a philosopher warns us that we may be mistaken at least in some degree, that is that successful practical applications do not necessarily justify the claim that the pictures upon which they depend accurately portray some aspect of the world-as-it-is. Barnes declares, again we think quite prematurely, that 'all cultures stand symmetrically to this reality', that is that none is closer to it than any other. But that is precisely what they do not do. A flat earth representation and an oblate spheroid representation do not stand symmetrically to the figure of the earth. The Galenic principles and the roles Harvey assigned to the renal portal vein do not stand symmetrically to the human blood system. And so on. Of course if you were to task what the ancient and modern geographers compared their pictures of the earth with, Barnes and Bloor would remind you that it is not the earth, but perhaps the earth as seen from a space ship or as seen in a photograph, and that each of these 'seeings' is itself 'mediated by culture and language'. Those of us who have successfully flown around the world, or taken a trip in Concorde and seen the curvature of the earth with our own eyes would be mightily unimpressed by this argument, since we would be inclined to say that if we had a flat earther as our companion he or she would have been shaken by the experience.

Of course it is true that the more recondite branches of physics do postulate classes of beings very remote from those we encounter in common experience. But the Strong Programme is presented as a general account of science and must hold good as much for geological strata as it does for neutrinos.

Some Standard Objections to the Strong Programme

The four tenets, read in the light of single-barrelled realism, have each been the subject of criticism.

Objections to Tenet 1: The causality principle

Once 'states of the world' are admitted as part determinative of our beliefs the way is open to use Strong Programme analysis to identify social determinants of our beliefs, and so systematically to delete them from our grounds for accepting certain claims as sound knowledge of the natural world. We would delete the effect of social 'pressures' on believers in just the same way as we delete irrational prejudices and special pleadings when they come to our notice. We should treat just those errors that can be put down to defects in the equipment we are using. Of course we could never guarantee to have eliminated all determinants of belief other than the relevant states of the world. However by applying and reapplying our Strong Programme analysis we could make the residual social component in the grounds for any given belief vanishingly small. Of course we can never be sure that we have eliminated every trace of social determinants from our grounds for believing something. Even if we had achieved this we could never be sure that it had been achieved. So we must be content with single-barrelled realism. In short, though each team of investigators looks at nature through a cloud of prejudices and prior assumptions, and could never achieve full and true understanding of the natural world, it is perfectly possible that each reveals a different but genuine aspect of that world.

Objections to Tenet 2: The impartiality principle

According to this principle there must be a social explanation of why certain standards are treated as authoritative and certain procedures picked out as rational. We declare that a certain research programme has been successful and another has failed. These declarations need an explanation and part of that explanation will be social. But because we agree that something has been brought into being in whole or in part by social forces does not mean that it is itself just a social fact. We come to hold a true belief about the geography of a certain part of the world just because of the social forces brought to bear upon us. One might object that this interpretation of *Tenet 2* commits the product/process fallacy. The fact that the process by which something is brought into being has certain properties is not adequate grounds for ascribing those properties to the thing brought into being. It must be examined independently. A true belief can be shown to have been arrived at by any route at all, or none, without inpugning its truthfulness or falsehood in the slightest. The fact that a belief is established socially has nothing to do with whether it is true.

But perhaps the tenet should be glossed in a more radical way. Perhaps we should take it to be the claim that concepts of truth and rationality and their opposites, are social concepts. '. . . is true' simply means '. . . has been accepted by the power-elite of my thought-collective'. However this is not the position of the Strong Programme. Bloor himself (1976: 34) allows for three uses of the words 'true' and 'truth'. They can be used for expressing the claim that some belief shows how things are in the world. They can be used to register pragmatic success. Thirdly they have a rhetorical or persuasive function. Only the last of these is social, in the sense in which that concept is used by advocates of the Strong Programme.

Objections to Tenet 3: The symmetry principle

Laudan (1981) has argued that causal explanations are called for only when we wish to account for false beliefs. '. . . the sociology of knowledge may step in to explain beliefs if and only if those beliefs cannot be explained in terms of rational, intellectual history'. Presumably rational, intellectual history displays the premises from which the beliefs were drawn, and the principles of reasoning by which they were reached. However the Strong Programme advocates would have a very short way with this suggestion. A social element cannot be eliminated from any account which purports to explain why we have the concepts we do and the standards we actually apply, why one method of assessment counts as rational and has hegemony over all others.

Objections to Tenet 4: The reflexivity principle

It has been argued that this principle represents a fatal concession. It leads straight to paradox and self-refutation. For example Hesse (1980: 42) has argued:

Let P be the proposition 'All criteria of truth are relative to a local culture; hence nothing can be known to be true except in the sense of 'knowledge' and 'truth' that are also relative to that culture. Now if P is asserted as true, it must itself be true only in the sense of 'true' relative to a local culture (in this case ours). Hence there are no grounds for asserting P (or, incidentally, for asserting its contrary).

Of course, as Hesse herself points out, this argument fails since the 'grounds' referred to in the conclusion must be absolutist in the sense of being both foundationalist and objective, which is exactly what the Strong Programme denies can be found in any culture. So there is no culture, including ours, in which the paradox can be formulated. The Strong Programme is, like every other human proposal, something for which a case has to be made, well or ill, according to the standards of our place and time.

The Strong Programme Reconsidered

Perhaps Barnes and Bloor had something else in mind when they enunciated the Strong Programme, something of a more traditional philosophical cast. Could we decide whether a proposition was worthy of belief by making a comparison between something cognitive, a description, and something non-cognitive, the world-as-it-is? What would the basis for such a comparison be? It could only be between a model, a humanly constructed working representation of some aspect of reality, and a material state of affairs, *as perceived*. But the latter is also cognitive, or as Wittgenstein puts it, 'partakes of thought and partakes of sensation', being mediated by concepts, immanent in the uses of language. So in the end the Strong Programme rests on a foundation in the cognitive psychology of perception (Manicas and Rosenberg, 1988). Acts of perception are tests of hypotheses. Why should we believe that? Is it not because of a certain historically and linguistically conditioned use of quite specific and local criteria, those in use in contemporary psychology of perception? And so the cycle begins again. But at least this shows that the Strong Programme is not innocent of ontological presuppositions.

However a familiar and long-standing objection can be made to the radical way the world-as-it-is and the world-as-it-appears-to-be are ontologically and epistemologically demarcated. The world must actually have the power to bring about the effects that we call sensory or perceptual experience. Of course the human response is not a transparent window through which to view the world-as-it-is. However it is hard to deny the minimalist assumption that the dispositions displayed in the reactions of instruments and people are real properties of the world and are as they seem to be. Some refinement of this notion is in order, since which of all its range of dispositions and powers the world manifests to people will depend on how the human senses are constituted and the kinds of experimental equipment we have so far managed to make.

In what sense then is the Strong Programme relativist? Though Strong Programme advocates deny the possibility of sharing individual experience, the root of the old epistemology, they emphasize the importance of the possibility of communication which allows for the development of a *universal* community of knowledge. Strong Programme epistemology is *antifoundationalist* in that it rejects the idea that the grounding of knowledge is in some primitive level of experience. However Barnes and Bloor allow for, indeed insist upon a role for the world-in-itself in the causation of belief. Provided we tidy up the Strong

Programme metaphysics by insisting upon a dispositionalist ontology there is a kind of *foundationalism* to be
discerned in their position. Real dispositions are displayed
in the reactions of instruments and human beings. Finally
we must ask about the objectivist element in the Strong
Programme. It is with respect to this issue that the
Programme is at its most relativist. There is no experience, individual or collective, that is unmediated by the
products of culture, language and other representational
devices. Even the dispositionalist must acknowledge that
the terms in which their powers and dispositions are
described are drawn not from the state of the world
grounding the dispositions, but from the effects of those
powers and dispositions on things within the human
world. And that is to acknowledge the mediation of
culture. The Strong Programme is antiobjectivist.

What the Strong Programme brings to the debate
between absolutists and relativists is a clear and full
acknowledgment of the centrality of individualism in the
formulation of traditional epistemology. There is no
universal foundation for scientific knowledge to be found
in the elementary experiences of individual human beings.
In rejecting that assumption we must give a central role to
the thought-collectives in which knowledge is actually
brought into being.

Afterword

These arguments have not yet brought out the deep
underpinnings of epistemic relativism. It can be shown to
be a consequence of accepting both semantic and ontological relativism. If the expressions of a language are meaningful only relative to the culture in which it is used and

what exists is also dependent on that same culture then knowledge, the linguistic presentation of what there is, is relative to culture in a very strong sense. Another way of attacking epistemological relativism would be to combine the counter arguments we have developed against semantic relativism in chapter 2 with the arguments against ontological relativism that will be deployed in the next chapter. But none of these counterarguments is without weaknesses. We shall find that though we cannot recommend the arguments for relativism without qualification, we cannot whole-heartedly recommend their rebutting arguments either. It seems that while we cannot prove that all knowledge is relative to culture, we cannot prove either that we could obtain knowledge that *was* absolute, that is universal, foundational and objective!

4

Ontological Relativism

Introduction

Ontological relativists believe that what exists for human beings is relative to the concepts they possess and the procedures of enquiry with which their culture equips them. It follows that for different cultures there will be different catalogues of what there is. Ontological relativists are not saying that it is just what people believe exists that varies from culture to culture, but something much stronger, that what exists can only be said to exist for this or that culture. The major part of this chapter will be devoted to discussing the thesis of ontological relativism as it is applied in the context of the physical sciences and apropos of the material world. We shall also discuss, though less extensively the very much less dramatic application of the thesis of ontological relativity to artifacts, both material, such as melodies and works of art, and discursive, such as institutions. We shall arrive at a view of the ontology of the physical sciences that is neither strongly relativist nor strictly absolutist. If anything our position leans somewhat towards a highly qualified relativism.

There is a close tie between theses about the relativism of knowledge and ontological relativism. In chapter 3 we showed how in debates about the status of scientific and other kinds of knowledge of the natural world we must bear in mind that there are two main varieties of epistemic relativism.

(1)   *Protagorean relativism*: Cardinal Bellarmine held, on good grounds in his framework of concepts and procedures, that the universe is geocentric, while Galileo held on good grounds in his framework of concepts and procedures, that the universe is heliocentric. But the statements 'The universe is geocentric' and 'The universe is heliocentric' cannot be true together. As we have emphasized the very formulation of Protagorean relativism presupposes some degree of semantic absolutism, at least that there are some universal meanings. According to Protagorean relativism the impasse is resolved by declaring that each has his own truth. That such a resolution is called for presupposes some degree of semantic universality, in that there is only something to resolve, if terms like 'moon', 'geocentric' and so on have a shared meaning.

(2)   *Fleckian relativism*: There can be two propositions using the same vocable, both of which are locally acceptable, but in which that vocable has diverse meanings in each local system or 'thought-style'. The AIDS establishment holds that HIV is the cause of AIDS, while some sceptics hold that depression is the cause of AIDS. One way of resolving the seeming impasse is to agree that the vocable 'AIDS' has one meaning in the establishment thought-style and another meaning in the thought-style of the sceptics. For the former group it is defined as that syndrome (or set of symptoms), including those of Karposi's sarcoma, which are observed in HIV positive patients; for the latter group 'AIDS' is the word for a similar set of symptoms or syndrome, including the symptoms of Karposi's sarcoma, whether or not the

patient is HIV positive. The meaning of the vocable, 'AIDS', must be different in each case.

It is important to keep in mind that Protagorean relativism can obtain for two propositions only if Fleckian relativism does not obtain for any of their constituent concepts. Two propositions can be related by contradiction or contrariety only if their common terms have the same meanings in each proposition. Fleckian relativism, summed up in the idea of incommensurable propositions, suspends debate in favour of efforts at conversion. We cannot debate across thought-styles. We can only attempt to convert the adherents of the other way of thought to our own.

We could express the idea of ontological relativism in this thesis: it is coherent, in all scientifically significant cases, to judge a well-specified entity as existing relative to one version of reality as expressed in some symbolic system/language but as not existing relative to some other version of reality. The notion of 'version' is drawn from Goodman's (1978) *Ways of world making*. A version of reality consists of all those classes of beings whose existence is required to make the use of a certain symbol system intelligible. Bearing in mind the distinction between Pythagorean and Fleckian relativism, we can see that if ontological relativism were conceived in a Fleckian mode there could be no debate. There must at least be a sufficient system of common meanings to specify the same thing in both systems, even though in one its existence is denied while it is affirmed in the other. If world versions were absolutely incommensurable then ontological relativity could not even be formulated. We could not then say that something existed for us but not for them, since we could have no access to the world versions of the others.

Must ontological debate then simply collapse into a listing of version-relative catalogues of existents? Could we not ask whether some versions of the world are better than others, in the sense of being 'righter'? And then give our allegiance to the existents of the better version? Goodman claims to be a 'radical relativist with restraints'. The restraints turn out to be implicit in the admission that the question of the relative rightness of versions makes sense. While he is unwilling to carry what for him is the dispensable burden of a full scientific realism, that is the doctrine that by the use of the methods of science we can come to know of things which we cannot observe, he wishes to retain something of the idea of the 'progress of science'. But, according to Goodman, no 'world' independent of one's symbol systems is accessible, so it cannot play any role in our cognitive judgements even if it existed. Truth or more broadly rightness, must be a feature of the internal relations within symbol systems. Rightness of a version cannot be determined by how closely it matches a pre-existing and independently known world.

As we shall show in the course of this chapter, the seeming intractability of the questions as they cluster around the application of the absolute-relative distinction as it appears in ontology, is due in large part to the assumption that only all-or-nothing answers will do. There is a via media and we shall find it in the philosophy of science of Niels Bohr.

Some Arguments for Ontological Relativism

Existence and versions

Goodman's argument can be laid out as follows:

Only the accessible counts as real
What is accessible is relative to versions
therefore
What is real is relative to versions.

Goodman resists the idea that there is a place for the concept of a world independent of world-versions and hence common to all world-versions. Even if the idea is intelligible such a world would be inaccessible, and on this account could do no philosophical work. So the 'rightness' that he admits that may distinguish versions cannot be understood as a comparison between versions and a version-independent reality, since that comparison cannot be made. However he does keep open the possibility for critical discussion about the rightness of certain world-versions by speaking of the fittingness of their parts in relation to one another as they emerge. He tells us that world-versions are formed through the transformations of previous world-versions by composition, decomposition, weighting, deletion, supplementation, deformation, and the like. He says

> Has a constellation been there as long as the stars that compose it, or did it come into being only when selected and designated? In the latter case, the constellation was created by a version. And what could be meant by saying that the constellation was always there, before any version? Does this mean that all configurations of stars whatever are always constellations whether or not picked out and designated as such? I suggest that to say that all configurations are constellations is in effect to say that none are: that a constellation becomes such only through being chosen from among all configurations, much as a class becomes a kind only through being distinguished, according to some principle, from other classes.

Now as we thus make constellations by picking them out and putting together certain stars rather than others, so we make stars by drawing certain boundaries rather than others. Nothing dictates whether the skies shall be marked off into constellations or other objects. We have to make what we find, be it the Great Dipper, Sirius, food, fuel, or a stereo system. Still, if stars like constellations are made by versions, how can the stars have been there aeons before all versions? Plainly, through being made by a version that puts the stars much earlier than itself in its own space-time (Goodman: 1982: 33).

It seems to us that the key expression in this passage is not 'version' but 'made'. The trick is to slip in a change in the meaning of 'made' that leads to the thesis of ontological relativism. This change can be spotted in the list of artifacts, 'Great Dipper', 'Sirius', 'food' and 'stereo system'! Clearly the first and final items are artifacts. In an uncontroversial sense they are made. 'Food' may be made, like a cake, or found like an oyster. 'Sirius', millions of tons of burning hydrogen, is found like an oyster, not made like a stereo. Of course to find it I need the appropriate prescription, and that I get from my symbol system, my language and my astronomical sciences. Oysters are easily identified in my version of the biological world and in that same version they are edible. But they are in no sense *fabricated*. To make the existential point Goodman needs to merge the category of '*objet trouvé*' with that of 'manufactured object'. But pointing to the mere presence of symbol systems in both procedures does not serve to bind them into the kind of commonality the argument requires. The role of symbol systems is quite different in the two cases. In fabrication the symbol system specifies in advance what I shall make, and refers to something of the relevant ontology now existing where none existed before. Brunel designs a bridge which he imagines would span the Tay and then builds it. In finding a new star the symbol system specifies in advance what would satisfy the criteria for membership of a certain category, to be fulfilled, if at all, by something already existing.

Setting aside the weaknesses of Goodman's argument we can still usefully consider the question of the degree to which ontological categories are version sensitive, that is what would be abolished were a version to be abandoned. If a category is abolished does the thing categorized vanish? No, because categories are components of hierarchical systems. Should we decide that whales are not fish these great creatures do not disappear since our organic type hierarchy includes aquatic mammals. Only if the entire hierarchy of categories were to be abolished would the things go too. If we abandon stellar categories for field categories, stars go, but not their electromagnetic and gravitational fields. We would still have a use for the terms 'Sol', 'Betelgeuse' and so on. But why would we abolish a whole category system? Only if we already had independent evidence that the supposed manifold of beings which it had been used to classify did not exist! We abandon our search for the real basis of the distinction between 'seraphim' and 'cherubim' when we no longer believe in the existence of angels.

To see how we might rank ontological categories by reference to version-sensitivity consider again the controversial proposition

HIV causes AIDS

There are three categories of existents presupposed by users of this proposition: *viruses*, *causal mechanisms* by which an instantiation of the viral concept affects the body in such a way as to produce the observable features of the disease, and *symptoms*. Let us rank these categories with respect to their degree of 'version sensitivity'.

In the above proposition 'causes' specifies a type of productive mechanism the components of which and the processes in which are probably unobservable and known by such standard but version sensitive methods as model building and testing. Ontologically 'causes' refers to a type of process.

'AIDS' is a syndrome of disease presentations, that is a cluster of observable symptoms of various types. Ontologically 'AIDS', the AIDS syndrome, is a type of complex property.

'HIV' refers to a class of entities currently observable with powerful sense-extending instruments such as electron microscopes, and detectable by the chemical identification of characteristic antibodies. The use of these instruments and techniques involves a great deal of electromagnetic and particle theory, not to mention large tracts of organic chemistry. Ontologically the HIV virus is a type of object.

It seems clear that existence claims about processes, e.g. causal mechanisms, those which actually link viral infestation to disease symptoms, are more version sensitive than claims with respect to observable properties of persons, for example the symptoms of Karposi's sarcoma. Claims about things, for example viral particles, are the least version-sensitive. This follows directly from the relative ease with which the several claims to existence under each ontological category are defeated. Processes extend from the past into the future. We may think we have identified a process from a current glimpse of it, only to find that, in the future, it led somewhere other than where we expected. To claim that we know a certain process exists is rather hazardous. Properties involve dispositions. Their display depends on the obtaining of certain conditions, which again may, in the future, surprise us. To claim that we know that a certain disposition exists is also somewhat hazardous. But things are occurrent. They exist, if at all, in the here and now and offer fewer hostages to fortune. Of course we may change our minds as to what kind of thing something is, while we continue to believe in its existence. Are comets chunks of rock or conglomerates of ice and dust? Processes are more version-sensitive than dispositional properties, which, in turn, are more version sensitive than are material objects.

Suppose now we rank our candidates according to a different principle: namely, with respect to 'accessibility' to human observers. In this ranking the unobservable causal process will be the most version sensitive. It is more likely that we will abandon our belief in a hypothetical causal mechanism when we cease to believe the theory from which it was derived. In these circumstances, just as has happened in the real world of virology, 'HIV', the viral entity revealed by advanced empirical techniques, does not vanish with growing doubts about its role in the causation of AIDS. We still believe that the virus exists. The least version sensitive element in the 'HIV causes AIDS' proposition is 'AIDS', those observed properties of human beings we collect up in the syndrome of the disease. They will survive the abandonment of the belief in the existence of the alleged causal mechanism and even a loss of faith in the existence of the virus. In our example, the syndrome 'AIDS', the clustering of established but diverse disease entities under the new umbrella category is obviously version sensitive, as critics of the AIDS 'industry' have pointed out. But even if the medical profession ceased to believe in the composite disease AIDS, Karposi's sarcoma, for instance, would not cease to exist.

To make his case Goodman would have to show that the progression of version-sensitivities does not terminate in categories which are wholly version-insensitive. If such categories of beings existed they would be common to all versions.

Let us now sum up the argument by the use of our three classificatory categories. Goodman seems to have been claiming that specific ontological categories, for example 'star', are neither universal (that is play a role in all cultures), nor foundational (that is serve to pick out a set of ultimate beings into which all ontological categories could finally be analysed), nor objective (that is make sense when imagined to exist independently of any human cognitive activity whatever). While we are happy to accept that ontologies are neither foundational nor universal, Goodman's argument does not show that they are not objective (that is not there all along, waiting to be picked out).

Bhaskar (1975) has drawn attention to a persistent fallacy in the reasonings of relativists, even those as sophisticated as Goodman. It is fallacious to draw a negative ontological conclusion from the demonstration of a certain kind of epistemological limit. We may know of something without knowing it, in the sense of being acquainted with it. The fact that for some reason we cannot make the acquaintance of something does not entail that we cannot know of it, and so have some grounds for taking it to exist. We are entitled to draw positive ontological conclusions from epistemological successes, for example we believe in the existence of *terra australis* because Captain Cook made it known to us, by becoming acquainted with it. But the situation is not symmetrical. It might seem that from an epistemological failure we should be able to draw negative ontological conclusions. We search for something, fail to find it, and then conclude that it does not exist. This bit of reasoning is valid only if the type of being we seek is such that we could become acquainted with it, for example by touching it. But there are many other ways in which we might become convinced that something exists than that. In some cases we know that no matter how we search the being in question is not of the kind with which we can become acquainted. If the theory of quarks is correct we might believe in their existence knowing that they could never appear other than bound into subatomic particles.

There are two grounds for Bhaskar's contention. The first ground is the moving boundary argument. What is unknowable at this moment may become knowable at another time, because the boundary between what we can know (by acquaintance) and what we can know only indirectly and by inference shifts with developments in technology. It would be absurd to say that the moons of Jupiter were brought into being by the Galilean telescope that rendered them knowable, in the sense of visible. What we can observe out of all that exists is determined by the instruments we have available. The second ground is the cognitive analogue of the first. What we can identify and classify out of all that exists is determined by the classificatory system that we have in hand. In learning to identify rocks and to pick them out as 'shale', 'schist' and so on, we have to learn a system of geological classification. It would be absurd to say that learning a geological classification brings these rocks into being. While the first argument depends on the fact that the boundary between what can be observed and what cannot is historically contingent the second depends on the fact that the boundary between what can be conceived and what cannot is also historically contingent.

'Exist' and 'exist for ...'

The Protagorean relativist might offer us the expression 'exists for . . .' as the proper way to express a relativist existence claim. To assess this proposal let us compare 'Bacteria exist for Pasteur but not for Aristotle' with 'Bacteria existed all along, too minute for Aristotle to observe, but were eventually revealed to Pasteur by the use of the microscope'. If we accept the propriety of the former account of the ontological status of bacteria we should be relativizing existence to the beliefs and exploratory capacities of individuals. The example presumes that Aristotle and Pasteur might have shared criteria as to what is to count as a bacterium, so that this case differs from the case in which an existence claim cannot even be made because the explorers in question do not share an idea of the kind of object in question. By what argument could one look for support for such a seemingly implausible thesis as that all existence is 'existence for . . . '?

The late R. L. Goodstein was famous amongst his friends for the following argument: experience teaches that the visible presence and visible absence of bacteria are correlated with the presence and absence of microscopes. One never finds bacteria without there being a microscope involved. So by Mill's methods of agreement and difference microscopes must be the cause or part of the cause of the existence of bacteria. So existence is relative to the equipment available. By the same argument the moons of Jupiter are brought into being by Galileo's use of his telescope, with which their existence is well correlated empirically. One finds a somewhat similar argument deployed by van Fraassen (1980), in his attempt to relativize existence to what can be perceived with the naked eye.

A counter-argument to Goodstein's move can be mounted in a familiar anti-Humean style. According to Hume the only empirical elements in the causal relation are contiguity and concomitance, the necessity we seem to see there being a projection of the psychological phenomenon of habit engendered expectation. By way of reply one can show that this leaves the distinction between accidental and causal sequences unexplained. The distinction is made in scientific practice by supposing that in the latter case there are causal mechanisms at work while there are none in the former. In many cases these mechanisms are unobservable. They are not inaccessible in Goodstein's strong sense, since we have powerful symbolic systems for describing what they might be like. Combining this insight with the moving boundary argument is enough to block Goodstein's against the thesis that what I see with the help of a microscope was there all along, waiting to be brought to light by being made visible. Whether something is observable *ab initio* depends on historical contingencies. Does a relativist seriously expect us to suppose that the potsherd dug up in an archaeological excavation was not there all along waiting to be found? Would its ontological status have been different if it had been lying on the surface for millennia, glanced at each day by passing shepherds?

Grammatically 'existing . . .' and 'existing for . . .' are distinct, in such a way that the latter cannot step into the place of the former. If a viviparous fish exists it may or may not exist for Aristotle. It depends on whether he spent some of his time on Lesbos studying dogfish.

'Existing' does not imply 'existing for'. Nor does 'existing for' imply 'existing'. We can say that the crystalline spheres existed for Aristotle since we have reason to think that he believed in them. But a report on Aristotle's state of mind concerning the heavenly spheres, though not wholly irrelevant to whether we think they exist, certainly does not entail anything about the independent state of the cosmos.

The crystalline spheres were unobservables. Should we believe in the existence of something that Aristotle believed existed because he had observed it? The route from something that existed for Aristotle in this sense to something existing for us is complicated because it involves the question 'existing as what?' The great statue of Athena existed for Aristotle as a potent symbol of Athenian identity. But it does not so exist for us. Is it the same statue? In one sense it is. For both Aristotle and ourselves it is a material thing made of gold and ivory. In another sense it is not. For us it is a historical curiosity. A realist can concede that whether or not something exemplifies a type is a matter of the available concepts without compromising realism in general, that is that there are core existents, that may exemplify one type when considered in one framework and another in another. In a sense one and the same thing can come under more than one description.

We have come to a familiar impasse in our investigations. The arguments do not seem to be quite strong enough on either side to settle the matter. Is existence relative to instruments, categories and techniques? Or can we say that there are beings which exist quite independently of anything human? In each context that we have studied in earlier chapters, we have found that there are some considerations that favour relativism and some that do not.

Our way of resolving this impasse has been to distinguish the three varieties of absolutism; universalism,
objectivism and foundationalism. Arguments in favour of
the universality of some meanings and some forms of
knowledge can coexist with arguments against foundationalism, that is arguments against the thesis that all
meanings are reducible to some basic set of root meanings.
But the arguments for and against relativizing existence to
culture, language or technique cannot be so neatly partitioned out. Material existence is either universal, objective, foundational or it is none of these things. It seems that
either there is just one world of which each human being
has a partial and idiosyncratic view, or there are many, one
world for each culture, and, if the argument is pressed,
one world for each human being. Goodman's attempt to
straddle this dilemma seems unnecessarily tortuous. While
not denying that there is a material world independent of
our culturally relative versions, his argument is meant to
show that the idea plays no role in our practices. But as we
shall see in the next section, in a larger sense the idea is
indispensable.

Possible Resolutions

Two roles for the world

We may distinguish two uses of the idea of a 'world', one
criteriological, and one *regulative*. When someone argues
that a hypothesis is true because it corresponds to (a part
of) the world to some degree, when a truth-value is
assigned to particular hypotheses in virtue of the obtaining
of this relation, they are using the idea of the world
criteriologically. Alternatively, when one characterizes the

rationale or the point of a cognitive inquiry *as a whole*, by positing an independent world, the idea of the world is being used *regulatively*.

Now the criteriological use of the idea of an independently existing world is unacceptable to the relativist because it presumes that the basic or protocol statements which are to serve as evidence for more general claims to natural knowledge correspond to version independent aspects of that world. There are two problems with this idea. How can something to which we do not now have access serve a criteriological role? And can we make sense of the idea that a statement is true if it matches a state of affairs?

Let us look first at the idea of truth-as-correspondence. Broadly speaking two very different solutions have been offered to the problem of how such a correspondence could be made sense of. In his *Tractatus logico-philosophicus* Wittgenstein proposed a simple and elegant account of truth. Sentences are ordered sequences of words, and states of affairs are ordered sequences of objects. If we analyse sentences into structures of elementary names and states of affairs into structures of elementary objects, and each elementary name corresponds to an elementary object, then a sentence is true of a state of affairs if it is structurally isomorphic with it. Such isomorphisms are possible because the names in sentences are also objects. Sentences, in the sense of conglomerates of objects, are part of the world that they describe. This is the simplest account of truth-as-correspondence that one could imagine.

Another way of making sense of the idea of a words-to-world match is to make states of affairs language-like. If we say that true statements match facts, but facts are like statements then the 'matching' relation is logical. This kind of matching of words to world has come to be called 'coherence'. How could it be thought that states of affairs are statement-like? A physical set up has to be interpreted using some locally valid conceptual system in order to stand as a fact. To see that it is twelve o'clock by looking at the hands of my watch is to read it, much as one might literally read 'It is 12 noon.' The face of the watch and the sentence just quoted are ways of expressing the same cognitive content.

It seems that the coherence account of what it means to say that a statement is true is more readily construed in relativist terms than the correspondence account. If indeed a physical set-up can serve an epistemic role only if it is interpreted according to some conceptual scheme, then the variety of such schemes introduces a measure of relativism into the story. Of course it is not radical relativism since there is a physical set-up that is to be 'read'. The world functions criteriologically to constrain the range of possible readings.

What of the strong correspondence theory as proposed by the youthful Wittgenstein? He realized that a complete account of how words could be used to describe the world could not be given in language. One could never say that the name 'N' corresponded to the object O, because the object does not appear in the sentence, '"N" names O'. What there is in the sentence is the *word* 'O', which is just another name for the object. To solve this problem he introduced his now famous distinction between saying and showing. Such a relation as 'N' to O, the latter free of quotation marks can only be pointed out, shown. It cannot be said. This presumes independent access to the world of beings like O. Wittgenstein thought that language could only have determinate sense if there were indeed such elementary objects as would give sense to the elementary names of a language, but he never succeeded in delineating clearly what these were. If there is no given set of elementary objects the criteriological use of a version-independent world seems to be impossible.

A relativist might, however, make use of the thesis of metaphysical realism regulatively, that is make use of the idea that there is a material world existing independently of our knowledge of it to define the global project of the physical sciences. In this use the notion would help to make sense of what is phenomenally presented as a whole, without requiring independent epistemic access to every small corner of it. A relativist might concede that the project of the natural sciences makes sense only in the light of the assumption that there is a world existing independently of our conceptual systems, while insisting that all actual knowledge is version-relative.

On the other hand there might be a limited principle of version-relativism that would be acceptable to an anti-relativist, one which made use only of the notion of an interpreted world. We shall borrow the term *umwelt* from ethology to express this idea. In biology the term 'umwelt' is used for the free space in which each species makes its bioenvironment. For human beings the umwelt is part only of the larger physical world of space and time, that part available to the human species and human exploratory equipment. Since salmon can make no use of the land, nor does it figure in what they can perceive of the world, it forms no part of their umwelt. For human beings there are many umwelten, of different extents and limits. We shall use the term 'umwelt' then for the world as it is given to me and those who share my concepts, my knowledge and my equipment. It follows that there are wide varieties of human umwelten, though each is a part of the one physical world.

Human umwelten could have more than a regulative role in the development of natural knowledge. They could have a criteriological role. We do not need any more than a locally available slice of the world to help us to decide for and against the acceptance of this or that empirical proposition.

The world, of which each umwelt is a version could have only a regulative role when a philosopher came to try to give an account of the point of science-as-a-whole. For example it could be argued that each umwelt is drawn from the world-as-a-whole. The heavens as revealed by optical telescopes and as revealed by radiotelescopes are aspects of the one universe. However it is umwelten that are called upon to play any role in the material practices with which we try to make assessment of claims to knowledge or to belief-worthiness. The same holds for practical knowledge that has to be acted upon in our daily commerce with the world. It is the microbiologist's umwelt, just a small part of the world, that is revealed by electromicroscopy and that is criteriological in microbiology.

We can use our three varieties of absolutism as a protocol for setting out the status of the two rival world assumptions. An ontology in which the notion of 'the world' was used regulatively and the notion of 'umwelten' was used criteriologically would be objective, that is it would presume that there is only one world in question. But it would not be foundational, since it would be only against states of this or that umwelt that the propositions of science would from time to time be judged. Nor would that ontology be universalist. Each era has its own and proper point of view on the world, its own proper umwelt, against which it measures the viability of its practices and the truth of its beliefs.

The world does exist independently of those human arrangements that force the one and only real world to manifest itself in different ways in different conditions. The temperature of iron was assessed in old fashioned foundries by its colour, and in modern ones by a radiation detector. Each records a particular and different manifestation of a common state of the world, the degree of molecular motion in the ingot. Colour manifests itself only to animate sensibility, radiation manifests itself to a bolometer. The fact that there are many ways in which molecular motion manifests itself does not show that the temperature of a pool of molten iron is not a real property of a common and independent world, though it is never manifested as such. And its manifestations are always dependent on the prevailing conditions.

An updated interpretation of Bohr's philosophy of science

Bohr's (1963) enigmatic writings on the philosophy of science have greatly exercised scholars bent on bringing forth a coherent exegesis. In what follows we are concerned more to use some of Bohr's ideas as a spring board for sketching a middle way between the extremes of ontological relativism (there is nothing but versions) and ontological absolutism (there is one and only one world and it is given to us in the sciences) than to give a definitive account of what Bohr had in mind.

At the back of Bohr's thought there seems to have been the idea that the world is indefinitely complex and capable of displaying a huge variety of aspects of itself, depending on the way that it is approached and experimented with. None of the actual properties in which the world reveals itself are identical with the properties of the world as it is independently of the situations and set-ups in which various and different aspects of its character are manifested. In the traditional Lockean way of classifying properties it is only secondary properties of the material world that are revealed in experiments and observations. All we ever experience are effects of certain powers and dispositions of world-apparatus or world-people combinations. On the basis of this experience all we can properly ascribe to the world are powers to produce this or that effect in us or in our apparatus. All we say about the world must take a conditional form. If certain conditions are fulfilled the world will (or could) manifest itself in this or that way.

These conditional ascriptions will take the form of the attributions of dispositions to the relevant material systems, part humanly devised and part constituted by the interacting world: 'If a is in C then a will manifest M'. In this formula a is not some isolated and independent fragment of the world, but a composite being consisting of the person or apparatus and the world in intimate and indissoluble union. Of course both person and apparatus are in the world, but in the naive realist interpretation of scientific observation and experiment they are assumed to be transparent windows onto components and states of the world 'itself'. Neither the occurrent state of an instrument, the reading it displays at a particular moment, nor the experience of a person in interaction with the world, is to be construed as a glimpse of an occurrent state of the world. The states of instruments brought into being in experiments, and the experiences of people brought into being in perception are the results of the activation of material dispositions in the system being measured and the things and events being observed. We say that the state of a manometer (an instrument for measuring pressure) is caused by the pressure of the gas. But what is pressure but a disposition in a gas to bring about such changes in the state of manometers? But to what is the disposition to be attributed? According to Bohr's point of view, not to the gas alone, but to the total set-up, gas sample and manometer and whatever else is involved, all taken together. Similarly the track in a cloud chamber is a manifestation of electronhood that is available to human beings only in the context of that cloud chamber. It is the world and the cloud chamber that has a disposition to display itself as electron-tracks. What of the electrons that we picture as causing the tracks? They too are but affordances of the total set-up.

It follows immediately that which way the world is manifested to a human being, of all the possible ways the world could display itself, depends on which instrument is used to bring forth that disposition. The same point is germane to the interpretation of what we know by ordinary sensory observation.

A manifestation (phenomenon) cannot be partitioned into a bit due to the instrument *and* a bit due to the world. Only in the environment of that instrument is that disposition revealed that way, e.g. electric charge as manifested in an electroscope, or as manifested in a vacuum discharge etc. Thus these dispositions must be attributed to the instrument/world complex. Instruments are human constructions. It has been customary to borrow a term from the psychology of perception, a term due to J. J. Gibson (1966). We shall say that person/world and instrument/world complexes *afford* this or that observation or result to the person observing or experimenting. Of course the full story is even more complex than this. The results of experiments as recorded by instruments have themselves to be observed by people, so that we must say that in the end the result of an experiment is something that a person/instrument complex affords. For our purposes in this chapter we need only go so far as to emphasize that affordances are conceptually tied in with the kind of instrument or the sense modality, that is sight, touch, hearing and so on with which a human being has chosen to observe them. Cloud chambers afford tracks, just as electroscopes afford divergences of gold leaves, and Stern-Gerlach apparatuses afford split images.

We can now give an account of Bohr's two famous principles.

(1) *The correspondence principle*: All affordances which could be read by people must have an observable manifestation. (In quantum mechanics the manifestations of all affordances must be describable in the terms and concepts of classical physics.)

(2) *The complementarity principle*: Affordances may be such that they cannot both be manifested at the same time at the same place. For instance if something looks red at some time and place, it cannot at the same time and place also look green.

We say that hues red, green and so on are determinates under the same determinable, 'colour'. Other affordances can be manifested together. If something weighs 10 grams it can also be red. Pairs of this sort are determinates from different determinables. Whatever its colour a thing can have a certain weight, shape and so on. But it cannot have different colours, weights, shapes and so on at the same place and at the same time. If M_1 and M_2 are determinates under the same determinable, if a manifests M_1 then it cannot manifest M_2 at the same place and time. But if they are determinates under different determinables then they can be manifested together. In quantum mechanics it turns out that there are important prohibitions on the joint manifestation of determinates under pairs of different determinables. Momentum and position are just such a pair of determinables. The joint manifestations of affordances of ordinary things are restricted only by the rule that forbids joint manifestation of determinates under the same determinable. In quantum mechanics the restriction extends to the joint manifestation of certain determinables, for example, position and momentum.

Bohr's philosophy of science makes 'hard edged' or definite existence claims only for the affordances of apparatus/world complexes. There is a definite question as to whether this or that apparatus-world set-up can afford this or that manifestation, that is this or that measurement result, for instance.

Do affordances form part of an absolutist or of a relativist point of view in the ontology of physics? Once again the question when posed in this all or nothing way seems to be incapable of a coherent answer. However, we can assess the degree to which Bohrian affordances are in keeping with absolutism and with relativism by making use of our subclassifications within the generic category of the absolute. We find that they are nicely placed between the universal, objective and foundational requirements of the absolutists and yet have something of the contextual sensitivity that relativists have argued for.

1   Affordances are *non-universal*, that is they are not the same in all situations, but they are not ephemeral. An electron always affords a track in a cloud chamber and a click in a geiger counter.

2   Affordances are *non-objective*, that is they depend on which apparatus an electron is interacting with. But they are not subjective. They are public material properties or manifestations of the apparatus/world complex that exists at that moment. Experimenters can agree on the readings of instruments and the observations a competent observer ought to make in a certain physical set-up.

3   Affordances are *non-foundational*, that is other affordances which explain those could be found with the invention of new apparatus, but they do have a fixed role as test results for a particular set-up, that is they are not epistemologically irrelevant.

Ontological Relativism and its Epistemic Groundings

While the absolutist holds that progress in knowledge should be measured in terms of standards independent of the stage of a given inquiry, once the existence of some class of beings (neutrinos) or a unique object (Pluto) has been established it cannot be revised out of existence, relativists hold that this requirement is too strong. We can and sometimes do stop believing that a certain class of beings exists, and we may even abandon belief in a particular. No one now believes Weismann's 'gemules' nor do astronomers include Vulcan in their catalogue of the planets (*pace* Mr. Spock). But is it really true that there is nothing that later discoveries and subsequent revisions of theory may not delete from the cosmic scene? For relativists all knowledge, including knowledge of existence, is progressive with respect to provisionally accepted conditions of adequacy. One can speak of the growth or

decrement and deletion of categories of established existents, only in such relative terms. But what of the persons
who hold these views and the common objects with which
they manage their daily lives, for instance the very pen
with which a relativist sets down the thesis that all
existence is version-relative? Could the progress of knowledge and technique force us to delete people and their
pens as categories of existents? Plainly not, on pain of
paradox.

But how would an absolutist establish that the provisionally accepted standards of adequacy for existential
judgements did converge on a catalogue of universal,
objective and foundational existents? Only by establishing
that there were universal, objective and foundational
standards of adequacy for making existential judgements.

At this point in the discussion we must turn away from
the question of the relativity of existence to the relativity
of knowledge itself. An absolutist might insist, as does
Siegel (1987), that there must always be non-question
begging ways of settling cognitive disputes. But at the
heart of this very claim, according to the relativist, there
seems to be no non-question-begging way of settling the
meta-dispute, no non-question-begging way of settling
the dispute between relativists and absolutists. We *do*
discriminate between better and worse scientific theories,
better and worse histories of the American colonies, and
so on. By and large, there is a remarkable degree of
convergence of the views of working scientists and historians about the exemplars of success and failure in the
garnering of knowledge, in the criteria of good and bad
work. The absolutist assumes that where there is convergence there exists a point toward which such convergence
ultimately tends. But the only evidence we would have for
the positing of the real possibility of a singular ontological

terminus *ad quem* would be just the convergence in question. The relativist tends to offer pragmatic accounts for local and epochal convergences reflecting short term and culturally restricted confidence in this or that package of knowledge garnering procedures. A relativist might be interested in the actual practices of knowledge and exist-ence evaluation in particular critical contexts, and, via a kind of comparative *conceptual anthropology*, seek the method of discrimination actually deployed.

This is the sort of assessment of methods of assessment that is currently going on in the controversy about the relation between HIV and AIDS. But to assess this piece of social science the credentials of the critical community actually making the appropriate discriminations are pre-sumed, since, in interesting cases, the assessors are members of that very community. Here the absolutist may press the question: Why countenance the claims of those practitioners to decide the matter empirically? More than the empirical description of practice is needed. Indeed, what qualifies practitioners if not that they are generally more informed about the way the world is independently of their practice? Without an absolute standard, the very idea of a qualified practitioner becomes incoherent. Yet the relativist asks, in turn, How can this be provided without falling into foundationalism? The entire discussion as we have set it out up till now is replicated in the question of the status of practitioners as authoritative judges of scientific value. Once again a resolution could be reached by the use of the distinction between criteriological and regulative uses of the concept of a material world. And, once again, such a resolution would highlight the need to free ourselves of the assump-tion that in ontological matters only all-or-nothing answers will do.

Realism and ontological relativism

The strongest claims for the possibility of obtaining progressive knowledge of the world as it exists independently of human concepts, works and wishes, are to be found in scientific realism. Realists hold that it is possible to make well-supported claims about the existence of entities, properties and processes that cannot be observed on the grounds of the efficacy of theories constructed according to the rigours of scientific method which invoke these beings. It has been often assumed that scientific realism opposes both epistemic and ontological relativism, that the affirmation of one entails the rejection of the other. This sharp opposition is linked to a certain preconception about how realism is to be construed. If the real is understood in terms that are in no way dependent upon or relative to any culturally contingent considerations then realism must stand in stark opposition to relativism. As we have argued the limits of what we can know by acquaintance does not limit what we are justified in believing exists. A sharp separation between the ontological and the epistemological reflects an important aspect of scientific realism as many have presented it. If our categories of reality are constructed within a plethora of culturally relative conceptual systems surely scientific realism is indefensible.

Our reading of Bohr's philosophy of science has allowed us to sail between the Scylla of an indefensible absolutism and the Charybdis of an implausible relativism. Other analyses of the nature of scientific knowledge-garnering have converged on the same conclusion. According to Margolis (1993b) there is nothing which bars the thought that that which is constructed as real within culturally defined contexts is also real in the sense of scientific realism. This intuition is somewhat akin to the conception of the ever changing human umwelt, which is nevertheless an aspect of reality. It is possible for an internalist, one who holds that all existential categories are created within theoretical contexts, to project these categories onto an external world, a world which exists independently of its being examined. From within an internalist framework, one can make intelligible the idea of something to which we can have no direct epistemic access. We can talk of the intelligibility and of the inaccessibility of a particular or of a type of entity in virtue of a well-constructed theory, which posits the existence of the relevant type or particular. That is we might argue that it is necessary to assume the existence of a certain class of entities so that the phenomena which we know to exist should be possible. If there are to be electro-magnetic interactions there must be virtual photons. If there are to be earthquakes there must be tectonic plates. By the same token one may hold to a theory of truth in terms of a correspondence between discursively constructed cognitive objects and some aspect of the world, yet agree that one has no direct access to the world-in-itself, and so no way of making judgements as to the truth of particular hypotheses about the world beyond all possible experience. Thus we arrive again at the idea of the existence of the world as a regulative principle.

A Paradox of Ontological Relativism

As we have seen in previous chapters the relativism of each domain engenders a paradox when we try to apply it to itself. Ontological relativism is no exception. According to that view what exists is a function of versions, so while Sirius exists in one version it does not exist in another. Every version is the product of the use of a distinctive symbolic system, and that requires that there be someone who is the user of that system, whom we shall call 'The First Speaker'. In every version pronounced by The First Speaker he or she must exist, since all First Speaker's utterances will be indexed to that person as the responsible speaker. There will be some versions in which there is a Second Speaker and some in which there is not. It is logically possible that amongst the indefinitely diverse versions spoken into being by Second Speaker using a symbolic system from his or her repertoire, there will be some versions in which First Speaker exists and others *in which First Speaker does not exist.* Second Speaker may not know, in some First Speaker versions, that First Speaker exists. For example a European historian in the course of giving an account of pre-Columbian social geography creates a version of Second Speaker's discourse in which First Speaker has no place. According to relativists such as Goodman neither First nor Second nor any other Speaker is privileged with respect to ontology. What holds for First Speaker then must also hold for Second Speaker, namely to include or omit reference to any Speakers other than themselves according to which version of reality is then adopted. Since ontology is relative to versions, says Goodman, Second Speaker exists in some versions spoken by First Speaker who must exist in each of his or her versions, but not in others. But Second Speaker exists in some of First Speaker's versions. There is no constraint on when Second Speaker can speak any particular version. Therefore it is possible that there are cases in which a version spoken by First Speaker in which Second Speaker exists will be matched by a version spoken by Second

Speaker in which First Speaker does not exist, and this is plainly paradoxical. Though we can be relativists about the existence of quarks we must be absolutists in at least two of our senses, about ourselves. As Descartes rightly pointed out one cannot meaningfully deny that one exists. Our belief in our own existence must be universal, held to in all contexts, foundational, basic to any judgement.

We find ourselves in the same position as Descartes after he had uttered '*Cogito ergo sum*'. He needed the clear and distinct idea of a benevolent God to break out of the circle of his own ideas. We have broken out of solipsism with our Bohrian compromise, in which versions and the world are intimately entangled, the idea of neither making sense without that of the other.

The Existence of Artifacts

A melody is a musical entity. The category of 'melody' is central to the ontology of music. Questions about the existence of melodies are raised, debated and settled routinely. Notions like plagiarism and pastiche, quotation and variation, central notions in the discourse *à propos* of melodies make sense only if 'melody' with its appropriate criteria of identity, its marks of individuation and so on is a robust ontological category. But as anyone who has been to the Peking Opera will testify the existence of melody is relative to culture and local musical conventions. Not every successive change in pitch is a melody even in Beijing. It looks as if 'melody' is a prime candidate for an ontological category that is truly relative in that the identification of a pitch and rhythm sequence as a melody is not universal, nor is it objective, for instance capable of being expressed in terms of acoustics, and it is certainly not foundational.

Generalizing this insight we might well want to say that works of art, in whatever medium, are ontologically relative. What is a heap of bricks is a work of art for the curators of the Tate Gallery, but not for most of the British gallery going public. What is a hospital plaster cast is a work of art for some, and so on. Anthropologists have found that the ability to read a set of marks as a picture is a locally inculcated cognitive skill. There is no native capacity to read a photograph, even of oneself, as a representation. It is to this broad class of artifacts that Margolis' account of ontological relativism applies rather well.

From identity to unicity: the abandonment of polarized disjunctions

Margolis wants to capitalize on the possibility that non-converging interpretations can be legitimately defended, not as an interim or tolerable condition approaching an ideal condition of full convergence, but rather as a condition that is itself *ideally* admissible. He holds that this condition reflects the nature of cultural entities and their interpretations. Margolis embraces the possibility that two incongruent interpretations might both be plausible, though neither are true in the bivalent sense, that is stand in contradictory opposition to one another. The question of bivalent truth characteristically does not arise in such discussions. The search for a true interpretation is formally available, though characteristically it is not pertinent. Rather, such other values as plausibility, aptness, and the like are the terms in which discussions of cultural entities are characteristically pursued. Incongruent interpretations may be simultaneously plausible. More than one 'cultural entity' may exist at the same place and the same time, even for the same people.

Margolis holds that there is no reason why one should restrict the 'cognitive', the 'epistemological' or the 'existential' to matters susceptible of assessment in bivalent terms. Correspondingly, there is no reason to restrict the notions of *good reason, rational defensibility* or *worthiness of belief* to a rigid all-or-nothing polarization. The principles of existential exclusion that dominate the ontology of the physical sciences may not have a useful role to play in the context of works or art, institutions and so on. Terms like plausibility, aptness, reasonableness, appropriateness, and the like, which do not stand in polar oppositions to their negations are more appropriate for setting up the ontology of artifacts. There is no reductive strategy, he believes, by the use of which such 'plausibility-type' values are reducible to bipolar concepts. Given this caveat, he tolerates competition between so-called *incongruent* (but not logically contradictory) interpretations. Incongruent interpretations are logically weaker than contradictory interpretations.

All this becomes clearer if we distinguish the principle of noncontradiction from the principle of excluded middle. According to the principle of non-contradiction it cannot be the case that P and not-P are true together, if the meaning of P is the same in both cases. But it is important to stress that this is a formal constraint. As such, the prior question of its applicability arises. That is, before the principle can be applied it must be determined that the appropriate conditions answer to P. This is by no means automatic. For example, borrowing an example from C.S. Peirce (1940), we can see how what initially appears to be contradictory might really not be so. 'This diamond is hard and this diamond is soft' is not contradictory, on Pierce's view, until some testing procedure is provided according to which hardness and softness can be determined. A method of application needs to be provided before the sentence in question actually answers to the formal condition of logical contradiction. Without such a method, the sentence is not contradictory. Only after decidability conditions are provided can the condition of logical contradiction be said to apply to the case at hand. Characteristically, on Margolis' view, it is just those decidability conditions that are contentious and may be incongruent in the case of works of art and other artifacts. It is not the case that a given object-of-interpretation as such simply either possesses or does not possess a given property, exists or does not exist, independently of the context and purpose of its assessment or our belief in its existence. There may be different interpretations assigning seemingly competing properties to some artifact, melodious or cacophonous, without these assessments being formally contradictory. The Dalai Lama's choir may intone tuneless dirges as heard in relation to one musical context, but be rich in significant melodies when heard in another.

The management of contextually sensitive attributions requires a special technique. Margolis calls this 'imputational interpretation'.

> There is no reason why, granting that criticism proceeds in an orderly way, practices cannot be sustained in which aesthetic designs are rigorously imputed to particular works when they cannot be determinately found in them. Also, if they may be imputed rather than found, there is no reason why incompatible designs cannot be jointly defended (Margolis, 1980: 160).

Since interpretations may impute properties to rather than just find them in works of art, there is no reason to think that incompatible imputations cannot be defended: a given work may be imputed different sets of properties in different ways. Here arises the question of the identity of imputed works, the central ontological question. In so far as works may be imputed different properties in different ways in different circumstances, one wonders whether or not the results of such imputation are sufficiently diverg-ent that one no longer has a basis for talking about different interpretations of *one* work as opposed to inter-pretations of *different* works. In the latter case, the con-dition of competition between the two interpretations does not obtain, and there would be no need to invoke the intuitionist principle of *tertium datur*, that there is a third upshot of assessing the epistemic value of statements, namely 'unproveable'. This latter condition amounts to an innocuous pluralism, from the point of the view of the defender of strict bivalence. However, Margolis wishes to hold on to the idea that under different imputations we may still talk of one work of art. (See his 1989, for example.) This is possible on the condition that there is in place a 'soft' notion of identity, of 'unicity', much as there is for a 'self' undergoing 'self-development'. While there is a self which changes and transforms, the notion of self-development is not an oxymoron. Between stages of development the self could not be self-identical in a strict Leibnizian sense, otherwise an autobiography would have to be treated as a story of many sequential selves. Self-development to be coherent requires a softer view of self-identity. The same kind of unicity obtains for the identity of a work of art: the 'same' work is imputed different properties and interpreted differently in different circum-stances. At least such a condition as unicity is required for competition between two interpretations of a 'given' work. The same notion has an obvious application to institutions, concrete like universities and abstract like codes of laws.

The question of unicity is closely tied to Margolis' view of the admissibility of incongruent interpretations, as evidenced in the parenthetical remarks in the following (1980: 164):

> Thus, musical interpretations A and B of Brahms's *Fourth Symphony* or literary interpretations A and B of *Hamlet* are incompatible in the straightforward sense that there is no interpretation C in which A and B can be combined. But that is not to say that A and B cannot both be plausible [that is coexist]. (The equivocation on 'A' and 'B' is benign enough.) When, therefore, I say that 'we allow seemingly incompatible accounts of a given work . . . to stand as confirmed,' l mean to draw attention . . . to the fact that the accounts in question would be incompatible construed in terms of a model of truth and falsity, but are not incompatible construed in terms of plausibility (Margolis, 1980: 164).

Problems with the Margolis interpretation of epistemic and ontological concepts

Judgements of unicity depend on the propriety of using concepts like appropriateness, aptness, plausibility and probability for identifying and individuating those properties which we are ready to ascribe to 'cultural objects'. But these concepts are of two different kinds. Some are merely ellipses for 'plausible with respect to truth', or 'probable with respect to truth.' Yet aptness and appropriateness do not suggest such a reading. These notions do seem especially pertinent when discussing properties to be imputed to cultural objects-of-interpretation. To say that such-and-such an interpretation is appropriate or apt need not invite one to say that it is true, whereas to say that an ascription is plausible is to suggest that it might be true. However we can still ask about the polarity of concepts like aptness and appropriateness. Does the claim that A was more apt a characterization of the United States' Senate than B, entail that B was therefore not more apt than A? It would seem that one could not hold both that A was more apt than B and that B was more apt than A whatever one meant by aptness. Even aptness and appropriateness may exhibit the exclusivity or bipolarity just considered. Margolis urges the view that we can make relative aptness discriminations. But we would need to be shown some kind of overarching measure that would at once be non-exclusive (non-bipolar) and also could perform the discriminatory task of assigning a value to A over B, or to B over A.

One must also have some concern about Margolis' characterization of his view that the thesis that incongruous interpretations are admissible is relativist: 'It takes little imagination to see that admitting that judgments which are incompatible on the model of assigning truth-values (true and false) may be jointly defended in terms of the assignment of other values is tantamount to the adoption of a form of relativism' Margolis, 1980: 160). However, the abandonment of bipolarity alone does not lead to relativism. One must add a commitment to the contextual dependence of decisions as to where on some continuum of degrees the relevant properties of an object lie. Only then do we have genuine relativism. Suppose we add this condition to the non-bipolar conceptual system in use in some context, say that for deciding on the existence of melodies, works of art, institutions and so on. Where do we stand in relation to our three defining characteristics of absolutism: universalism, objectivism and foundationalism? That there are melodies in the Peking Opera is clearly not a reflection of a universal musical ontology. Nor is the question of the existence of institutions one that could be settled objectively, that is without reference to the interpretations of conduct offered by the tribe in question. Nor is there any way that a foundational ontology could be arrived at such that it figured in all existential and valuational judgements in all contexts and with respect all classes of 'cultural objects'. However, while we must concede that cultural objects exist only relative to the discourses that permit us to identify, reflect upon and criticize them, the same is not true of the beings of the material world. The human umwelten are indeed diverse, but they are 'slices' of the world. In a sense all cultural objects are but momentary vortices in the flux of human history. What we can glimpse of the material world is a function of our cultural equipment, but those partial views are, when interpreted along the lines of Niels Bohr's philosophy of science, glimpses of an independent reality.

5

Moral Relativism

Introduction

There are many different local conceptions of what is morally good and many different systems of laws in which at least some of these conceptions are embedded. 'Tribes' differ over such matters as the moral propriety of corporal punishment, aborting foetuses, avoiding income tax and so on. Some of these differences reappear in the legal systems in force in this or that tribe. Moral relativists believe that many of these differences are irresolvable in moral terms. They believe that there are no universal moral standards to which all tribal moralities and tribal legal systems must be subject. Moral absolutists hold that there are some universal moral principles, mandatory independently of the wishes of human beings, which must be the foundation of all normative systems that purport to be moralities. Before we can examine these positions we must find a way of picking out moral edicts from merely prudential maxims and rules of thumb. To this end we turn to Kant's moral philosophy.

How we Might Distinguish Moralities from Practical Maxims

The categorical imperative as a criterion of 'the moral'

Kant's moral philosophy is grounded in the distinction between hypothetical and categorical imperatives. Hypothetical imperatives are rules for bringing about desired ends, and our reasons for obeying them echo the reasons we may have for wanting to realize just these ends. For example 'If you *want* to achieve a good degree, then you *must* study hard' is such an imperative. The second clause expresses a condition for the achievement of what is described as desirable in the first clause. Categorical imperatives, on the other hand, are mandatory quite independently of any particular wants, desires or wishes of any and all human actors. A categorical imperative would take the form 'As a human being, you must do your duty', regardless of what you might or might not want, or of what seem to be practical advantages and disadvantages.

If we are going to consider the pros and cons of moral relativism we must have a way of picking out those systems of rules and maxims which are to count as a morality. Perhaps we can make use of the Kantian categorical imperative in its various versions for this purpose. Though, no doubt, this use is not quite what Kant had in mind in formulating them they are readily adaptable to that end. Any way by which we could pick out moral principles in general ought to be sufficiently general to cover a variety of particular moral schemes. Kant derives his categorical imperative from the very nature of moral judgements. Therefore since all versions of the categorical imperative are derived from and express the necessary conditions for a judgement to be a moral judgement they are eminently suited to serve as criteria for distinguishing what are truly moral principles from practical maxims and prudential hints, all of which would be expressed hypothetically relative to some desired end.

Summed up briefly Kant's versions of the categorical imperative appear as two central principles.

1 *The principle of universality* requires that though particular moral judgements may be imperatives only to individuals any principle that is to count as a generic moral imperative must be applicable to everyone including he or she who makes it.[1]
2 *The principle of ends* requires that everyone be treated as an end in themselves never solely as a means to an end.

Taken as criteria the two principles could be used to pick out just those systems of assessment of actions, thoughts, rules and so on that are to be taken as moral systems. Such systems must be applicable equally to all human beings and, when applied, require the treatment of all persons as ends in themselves, never solely as means.

A universalistic assumption in the Kantian criterion

The Kantian versions of the categorical imperative, taken as criteria for what is to count as a moral system, are not content free. The moral content of these criteria appears in further reflection on what it means to say that human beings should be treated as ends-in-themselves. Any behaviour which tends to destroy or minimize personhood is contrary to the principle that all human beings should never be treated merely as means to an end but always as ends. A defence of the use of foetal tissue for research into Parkinsonism would have to turn on a demonstration of the non-personhood of the foetus and its value to beings who were incontrovertibly persons, though it is conceded of course that the entity which is sacrificed is human. Only personhood is morally protected. Persons can be used as means up to the point at which they would surrender or endanger their personhood. We have not yet said what that point would be. This seems to entail that the universe of beings to which any moral system whatever applies must be already given as a universe of persons. Intertribal questions would concern only whether or not this or that group of human beings counts or does not count as persons.

If we count as moral only those systems of norms that satisfy the Kantian criteria, each and every one must secure the moral protection of persons. The range of alternative normative systems one might cite as evidence for moral relativism, must be moralities, and so must involve at least one universal principle, that persons are morally protected. Here we have the first whiff of a paradox in the attempt to state moral relativism.

Further universalist assumptions on which moral relativism depends

According to moral relativism, what counts as a morally good or bad person, what counts as a virtuous or vicious action, what counts as a good or bad character, is relative to the particular culture in which that distinction is made. That there are distinctions to be drawn between people, between actions and between characters is a universal that is assumed by all moral relativisms. However for the purposes of this chapter we shall assume that it is the way these distinctions are drawn rather than the viability of the distinctions themselves that is at issue. Thus the question whether virtues may not be vices on the other bank of the river presumes that on both banks the tribes make a distinction between good and bad conduct, virtuous and vicious characters and so on. While it is conceded that everywhere there are moralities it is argued by the moral relativist that there are no universal standards of morality. Moral absolutism can be expressed in the claim that there are moral principles to which the actions and characters of all human beings must accord. If moral absolutism were true we could make trans or pan cultural and pan historical assessments of moral worth.

We shall discuss moral absolutism mostly as it is expressed in the form of moral realism. Moral realism is consciously modelled on one current form of scientific realism, that scientific hypotheses are true or false by virtue of the way the world is whether or not we can know it at a particular time and place. Moral realism is strongly universalist. If infanticide is a moral evil it is a moral evil everywhere and at all times. According to moral realists there are universal moral principles that guarantee moral worth, if it is guaranteed at all. In this respect moral realism is both objectivist, in that there are supposed to be moral principles independent of any particular form of human association. It is also foundationalist, since all local moral questions would ultimately have to be referred to these universal moral principles. It shares with scientific realism a certain caution in claiming that the current basis of judgements of the truth and falsity of moral principles are final and unrevisable. Like current forms of scientific realism which admit that the terminus of perfect truth may not be attainable while insisting that some scientific theories are better accounts of the world than others, moral realism is progressivist rather than dogmatic. It tries to descry the direction in which greater 'objectivity' of moral judgements might be found rather than attempting to specify the terminus of such a development. In short moral realists claim that we can know whether one moral system is better than another, even though the specification of a perfect moral system might elude us.

The use of Kant's categorical imperative as a source of criteria for deciding between morality and prudence depends on a prior categorizing of beings as persons and non-persons. Only if rules are person-preserving are they moral. Is this a moral distinction? If so it seems to lead to two versions of moral relativism. Two tribes may mutually define each other as non-persons. They may have the same moral system and simply apply it differentially, one way to themselves, another way to their neighbours. This is the sort of situation that occurs in racially motivated forms of discrimination. Or the two tribes may agree as to their common personhood but disagree as to what is to be defended morally. One may hold paedophilia to be an evil, another hold it to be morally neutral or even a good. Thus we get three versions of moral relativism:

1   Relativism of personhood to culture, with a common moral doctrine.
2   Relativism of moral doctrine to culture, with a common conception of personhood.
3   Relativism of both personhood and moral doctrine to culture.

Let us spell out these basic versions in a little more detail.

(1) *Person relativism*, the doctrine that not all human beings are persons, is sometimes defended on the ground of intellectual incapacities. Those humanoid creatures who

are incapable of generalizing their judgements beyond the immediate moment ought not to be counted as persons and so lack the moral protection immanent in the Kantian criteria. This is sometimes said of the geriatric and those suffering from Down's syndrome. Sometimes the judgement of person relativism is based on grounds of character and temperament. Those humanoid creatures who are happy-go-lucky, incapable of serious commitments, have been declared to be less than persons. This was once said of the detribalized Africans enslaved in the old American south.

(2)   *Moral relativism*, the doctrine that each tribe has its own local morality, which is not assessable from the point of view of any other tribe, is suggested by the fact that there appear to be many and diverse moral orders, each of which meets the criteria derived from Kant's categorical imperative. Moral diversity can take at least two forms:
  (a) There is no universal moral criterion by which these diverse moral orders, that is systems of moral maxims and standards of virtue, can themselves be assessed morally. (Of course they can be assessed according to many other criteria, pragmatically, economically etc.)
  (b) The same action, described in some neutral, non-moral terminology, can be adjudged good, morally worthy and so on according to the criteria of one moral order while it is adjudged wrong, morally unworthy and so on or morally neutral according to the criteria of another.

The very idea of moral relativism implies that it is the same action that is assessed one way in one system and another way in another. If there is no commonality at all between what is assessed differently in different moral orders we could scarcely speak of moral relativism, only of moral diversity. There is just a whiff of paradox about these observations. Are there ever phenomena which could properly be called human actions which did not involve, covertly perhaps, some valuational principles? Just to pick out something as an action already sets that activity in a moral context. People are held responsible for actions, *ceteris paribus*, but not for what merely happens. Actions do not just happen. Someone does them.

Some Arguments for Moral Relativism

Arguments for moral relativism would have to show that there can be two or more sets of maxims of conduct which are mutually exclusive, and yet which satisfy the criteria which we have derived from the Kantian categorical imperative.

Anthropological arguments

It was alleged by Boas (1928) and Benedict (1934) that there is a great variety of moral systems, according to which an action, describable in some neutral terminology, would attract differing moral assessments. But which of the many ways in which cultures differ are the significant or relevant ones for the relativist argument? The dimensions of difference that matters morally is identified by Boasians by the use of the principle of selectivity. 'Every human society everywhere has made . . . [a] selection in its cultural institutions. Each from the point of view of another ignores fundamentals and exploits irrelevancies.' (Benedict (1934: 24).) Thus some aspects of life are elaborated in one culture and ignored in another which elaborates its form of life elsewhere. There is no rationale to this according to the Boasians. The origin of these diverse elaborations as consequences of selectivity in what is taken to be morally central lies in the vagaries of history. It is easy to see how the thesis of selectivity leads to moral relativism. Another culture might select and elaborate the military virtues and base its moral assessments of people's actions by reference to them. Others might elaborate a moral order in which moral virtue was found in the arts of peace. In the absence of a transcendental argument from the conditions of human life in general by which a philosopher could reveal an overarching criterion of moral worth, we can slip straight into the Principle of Tolerance, that each culture's moral system is right for it.

The Boasians, argues Hatch (1983), used two lines of defence for the Principle of Tolerance. Empirical evidence could be marshalled in its favour. It was claimed that because there are differing moralities attached to the same (in some sense) practice in different societies we must accept the Principle of Tolerance. But that is a remarkably weak argument in the absence of any proof that no overarching moral principle could be arrived at according to which diverse moral systems could be assessed. For example we have argued that the Kantian transcendental deduction of the categorical imperative leads to two criteria, namely the universality of moral maxims and the moral protection of persons, that enable one to show that certain systems of values used in the assessment of people's behaviour are not moral systems.

The second line of defence for the Principle of Tolerance is an elaboration of the idea that a moral system is to be tolerated if it is right for that culture. But what exactly is it for a moral system to be 'right for a culture'? For the Boasians this amounted to the principle that the practical

value of a custom in the life of the tribe showed whether it
deserved or did not deserve the local moral accolade. If it
did, then the Principle of Tolerance protected it from
trans-cultural moral assessment. Polygyny might be morally right in a culture in which agricultural labour is at a
premium. It could be morally wrong in an industrial
society based on the nuclear family. But this defence falls
foul of the general principle that moral imperatives cannot
be derived from factual propositions. It could be said in
response to a Boasian defence of some local custom
thought morally offensive by outsiders that moral compromises are often forced on people by circumstances, for
example the cannibalism adopted by the survivors of an
aircrash in terrible country. But that does not alter the
moral quality of the acts. To suppose it does would be to
confuse Austin's category of excuses (it is wrong but
circumstances forced me to compromise) with his category of justifications (it is really right when properly
understood). Circumstances support excuses. They do not
serve as justifications. Moreover 'forced by circumstances'
suggests the relevance of some other, unspecified moral
good, which is of greater force, *ceteris paribus*, than the
good suspended by circumstances.

Ironically the Principle of Tolerance cannot itself be
used to establish moral relativism, since it is taken to be
the expression of an universal moral value, namely tolerance. So this form of moral relativism, even if its defences
were more robust, is self-defeating.

Radcliffe-Brown (1952) gave a much sharper focus to
the anthropological argument with a clearer and stronger
concept of practical value than the Boasians had developed. According to Radcliffe-Brown, institutions,
including moral systems, are responses to permanent
needs or local exigencies. This is not so different from

Harris's (1974) claims about the nutritional role of cannibalism amongst the Aztecs that led to his controversy with Sahlins (1978). Harris had argued that social customs had their roots in the ecology of the region occupied by a society. The swampy plain on which the city of Mexico was built was an environment low in protein resources. This persistent shortage of a vital food stuff was the origin of the elaborate cosmological cannibalism around which Aztec religious and civic rituals were organized. On the contrary, according to Sahlins Aztec cannibalism had a proper place in a cosmological/moral system, and its persistence in the culture had almost no prudential or instrumental value. In a virtuoso use of some gruesome mathematics he showed that the contribution of human flesh to the diet of the Aztecs was tiny. By establishing this point Sahlins left the explanatory field to an appropriate cultural/moral account of the practice and its place in Aztec life.

Instead of some vague notion of 'rightness' Radcliffe-Brown has the much more robust concept of 'necessary for social/biological survival'. Cultural practices 'exist and persist because they are part of the mechanism by which an orderly society maintains itself in existence' (Radcliffe-Brown, 1952: 152). By eliding the reason for the practice with the justification of the practice, we reach the principle of functional necessity. Practices which conform to the principle of functional necessity are necessarily beneficial since they promote the long term survival of the group that adheres to them. The awful Yunamuno, whose culturally embedded violence and cruelty are a hard case for Boasian toleration, are probably in danger of disappearing as a culture since their treachery and persistent warfare is not likely to be conducive to the long term survival of their moral order.

We shall need another line of argument to defeat this form of relativism, since it would lead to the crowning of a culture as acceptably moral just because it happens, at this time that it still exists. It also entails that cultures that have ceased to exist, such as Hellenistic Greece or classical China, must thereby be poorly rated morally. We might object that extrinsic circumstances can destroy civilizations which, *ceteris paribus*, were fit to exist. But this would hardly upset Radcliffe-Brown's basic theory which entails that a moral order which has persisted for some considerable time must be tolerated. Cross-cultural criticism could be made only on pragmatic or prudential grounds. One could criticize the Nazis for perpetrating the holocaust only on such pragmatic grounds as that in the long run it was bad for business. One would be required to praise Hindu cow-worship on the prudential grounds that it was especially appropriate for scratching a living in the ecological conditions of the Indian subcontinent, as Harris (1974) has argued. Yet these sorts of criticism seem both callous and irrelevant to the moral quality of the practices that are condemned or praised. Adopting Radcliffe-Brown's conception of 'rightness' would seem to disbar us from the moral realm altogether.

Philosophical arguments

The vast amount of writing on this topic by philosophers discourages one from undertaking anything like a 'literature survey'. Instead we shall set out what we take to be the range of possible arguments. It will turn out to be rather modest in scope. We shall discuss three arguments for moral relativism.

The first argument is based on the thesis that all moral judgements are indexical of the position of the speaker, the one who makes the judgement. This is a kind of narrow individualism: I am the sole legitimate judge of what is right for me since it is I who benefit or suffer from the consequences of my actions and those directed towards me. Since the situation of every human being is unique each inhabits his or her own moral universe, the coordination of which into social groups is a matter of negotiation and compromise. The views of the majority cannot override the fact that consequences are suffered by individuals. We note a grammatical version of this argument due to Harman (1977), in which he derives something like this position from the claim that every moral judgement includes an indexical expression.

Our second argument is based on the ubiquity in real life of moralities of honour. In an honour morality different moral demands are made on different classes of people, and everyone agrees on or accepts the total code. Servants, farm hands and so on and their masters/mistresses all accept a system of differential rights and obligations (for instance as exemplified in the film *The Shooting Party*, a scheme which once operated on a global scale in the feudal system). However there is a problem in using the Kantian criteria for determining whether a code of honour is a moral system. Codes of honour and feudal systems of reciprocal obligations fulfil Kant's first criterion only counter-factually – 'Were I an officer I would have to shoot myself for letting down the side' and 'Were I a batman I would take care of my officer in all circumstances'. Both officers and private soldiers and enlisted men are moral beings subject to moral imperatives, but the codes appropriate to each group differ.

We can find the same principles at work in the caste morality of India, and in the nineteenth century morality of Western Europe in which men and women, masters and servants fell under different moral imperatives and are ascribed different virtues and vices, but within the same moral system of reciprocal rights and duties. Characteristically these groupings are explained, when they are dominant, by reference to the intrinsic nature of the beings involved. (Lilian Pinkham, inventor of Medicinal Compound, still on sale after the Second World War, offered it as a specific for 'women's weakness'.) Children and adults as well as law-abiding people and the criminal classes have been so set apart in not so distant times. But there is one point of paramount importance – one does not *choose* to be a gentleman or a lady, as if other options were there for one's consideration. One is, so to say, 'elected' to the status. If one conceives oneself as choosing between being a gentleman and being a 'bounder' one is a bounder. To be a gentleman or a lady is not just to live according to the code but to live up to it. At the heart of moralities of honour is the idea that the moral life is not so much a life exhausted by the doing of one's duty and fulfilling one's obligations as of being just the sort of person who does their duty and fulfils their obligations. One's personhood is immanent in these practices. As Goffman (1963) pointed out the gentleman and the lady fear and resent humiliation, while the citizen fears and resents only unfairness. The role of trials, in which evidence of wrong doing is assessed rationally relative to a body of law, is taken over by duels, in which the issue is not the proof of or defence against accusations of guilt, but the demonstration of character, for that is always what is at stake in such moralities.

Moral reasoning is the resort of the cad. He *works out* what to do. The gentleman and the lady and the gentleman's gentleman *know* what to do.

In these cases there is just the one coherent moral system, but its application is differentiated. Women are emotional and irrational creatures, in the Victorian view of things, and though falling under the moral rules of Victorian society, are immune from certain levels of blame. In Austinian terminology this is a relativism by excuse. Women's honour and men's honour is different in many societies. For instance in the Muslim Sudan the loss of a woman's honour infects the honour of the whole family, while the loss of a man's honour infects only himself.

Moralities of honour are the most plausible candidates for the role of exemplars of a defensible moral relativism in which persons are preserved as such across systems but rights and duties differ, and are relative to what the person is. Harman (1977) has suggested that we can make sense of this sort of relativism of systems with conserved person-hood by arguing that while it might be rational for one person to accept a certain maxim as applying to him or herself, and not to others, the same attitude to the same maxim might be irrational for someone else.

Harman's response to the objection that whatever principle sorts people out with respect to the applicability of moral maxims must be a moral principle, is to try to make the escape clause non-moral. As we saw above he proposes that we should say that a moral demand applies to a person only if it is rational for that person to accept the hegemony of that demand. People may differ as to what they take it to be rational for them to accept as moral imperatives. But surely a moral demand applies to someone or to some class of persons whether or not they accept it. One does not escape moral censure for stealing one's pupils' ideas by refusing to accept that plagiarism is morally obnoxious. The principle of universalization applies even if it were rational for some people to reject a moral demand. Such 'rationality' could only be the rationality of a hypothetical imperative. This follows directly from the categorical imperative, one of whose clauses is the principle that whatever I take as a maxim must be capable of being treated as a universal moral law.

Our third argument turns on the existence of alternative systems of moral assessment. Whereas moralities of honour are relative because the one moral system is relativized in its application to persons of different categories, there remains the case in which the people and their actions are assessed with respect to the edicts and values of two incompatible moral systems. Consider the case of an 'Evil Empire'. Life in such a social order as the regime of the Khmer Rouge is managed according to a complex system of assessments of actions and thoughts, it disposes of sophisticated distinctions among characters. It recognizes subtle categories of virtues and vices. However we look across the river and we see that the citizens of this empire enjoy a life which we would say was characterized by slavery, perversions and institutionalized cruelty. There have been no shortage of Evil Empires. There was the Nazi Third Reich and its monstrous racial policies, the regime of Pol Pot and its slaughter of intellectuals, the Aztec Empire of meso-America and the ritual cannibalism that required the annual slaughter of thousands of slaves, and there is everyone's favourite monsters, the awful Yunamuno, delighting in treachery and murder! In these societies we do find, as a matter of fact, that in a queer way the Kantian criteria are satisfied. In Communist show trials the accused condemned themselves. It may even be that amongst the citizens there reigns something like the Kingdom of Ends, the principle of the moral protection of persons. It all depends on where the boundary between persons and non-persons is drawn. It seems as if moral relativism must countenance Evil Empires. Yet we have the strongest intuitions that such empires are evil. However if judgements of good and evil are local and internal to each social/moral system how can we justify the strength of our intuition that such empires are evil? Somewhere we must find another deeper principle than those embedded in the Kantian imperatives.

If there is a deeper principle it must have something to do with the division of the members of the species, *homo sapiens*, into persons and non-persons. The simplest response to the moral relativism of Evil Empires would be to insist on the principle that each and every member of the species is a person. But that is to do no more than repeat our intuition. We can offer no further argument in support of it.

Some Arguments for Moral Absolutism

Moral absolutism must be at least as diverse as the moral relativism to which it stands in opposition. It must oppose both the anthropologists' Principle of Tolerance and the claim that moral judgements are indexical either of person or of social category.

Moral realism

The most telling argument against moral relativism would be a convincing defence of moral realism. Moral realism takes a variety of forms but common to all is the idea that there are moral facts, not just moral opinions or intuitions or customs. Moral facts, if there are any, would be true and putative moral facts would be false, by reference to states of affairs existing independently of moral judgements. There are varieties of moral realism because there have been different views as to the nature and content of moral facts.

Arguments for moral realism take their start from a supposed parallel between moral realism and scientific realism. For example in Brink (1989) we find moral realism characterized as follows:

1   There are moral facts or truths
2   These facts or truths are not constituted by the evidence for them.

Moral propositions then are to be assessed by reference to states of affairs that exist independently of human beings, their beliefs, concepts and interests, in so far as these can be ascertained. In keeping with this characterization of moral realism the truth and falsity of moral propositions would be naturally construed in terms of a correspondence or lack of it between moral judgements and relevant states of affairs. Whether or not the judgement had actually been made would have no effect whatever on the state of affairs which would make it true or false, in particular the judgement would not be constitutive or part constitutive of the corresponding state of affairs. However the difficulty of establishing the credibility or implausibility of moral propositions solely in the light of what obtains in some domain independent of human beliefs and interest and yet which is supposed to be a moral domain, has promoted attempts to establish moral realism on the basis of a coherentist theory of truth. According to that theory a statement is true just in so far as it is logically coherent with the largest body of mutually coherent statements that the culture then disposes of. Brink points out (1989: 20) that moral realism is objectivist in the following sense: 'Not only does ethics concern matters of fact; it concerns facts that hold independently of anyone's beliefs about what is right or wrong'. Of course the onus is on the moral realist to say what classes of facts these might be.

Moral realism and the analogy with science

The doctrine of moral realism has been formulated on the same lines as one of the prevailing formulations of scientific realism. Just as the thesis of bivalence defines scientific realism as the doctrine that theoretical statements are true or false by virtue of the way the world is, so moral realism, in general, is the thesis that moral judgements are true or false by virtue of the way some 'moral reality' is (Griffin, 1986). This is a somewhat vague characterization, and we can sharpen it as follows:

1   On the analogy with scientific realism we could construct an 'argument to the best explanation' account. Moral realism, it is alleged, is the best explanation of certain indisputable facts, for instance that people who at one time disagree about the moral assessment of some person's actions can be brought to agree. It seems that there is some 'fact of the matter' that their agreement must reflect.
2   By induction over normative intuitions we might establish universal moral principles. In a similar way inductivists believe that we find support for universal laws of nature by induction over those cases where we have found them to be true or to give true predictions. If everyone who is not mad or misinformed as a matter of fact feels the same appreciation/revulsion at some

person's action, then this reaction can be taken as the expression of a true moral principle.

3   If it were possible to derive a moral principle from the very nature of moral judgement itself, then that principle must be one to which everyone who makes moral judgements must subscribe, regardless of the moral system they employ.

The third argument can be dismissed right away. It amounts to the Kantian derivation of the two main versions of the categorical imperative: the maxims of a normative system must be able to be applied as universal moral laws, and the norms of proper action must be such that persons are always treated as ends, never solely as means. But since an enormous variety of moral systems can meet these criteria the Kantian categorical imperative cannot be used to specify one true and right moral system out of those that meet its requirements. It cannot be the basis for a moral realism of the sort Griffin is after.

There is one form of moral realism that is also easily set aside. This is the idea that the relevant facts are what as a matter of fact each person likes. Nowell-Smith (1954) argued that in the end all value assessment can be reduced to individual expressions of taste, about which no further dispute is possible. One can't ask a carnivorous diner why they prefer beef to mutton, or a Vegan why they always choose soy bean curd in preference to whole wheat pasta. There are no reasons in the discussion of which a rational adjudication of taste differences could be made. While any taste preference can be expressed in what is true for this or that person it can only be contingent that there are expressions of matters of taste which are true for all humankind. So by our Kantian criteria expressions of personal taste cannot be the foundations of a morality.

If moral foundations cannot be found in what feels right, in moral intuitions of acceptable or unacceptable behaviour, the question remains: what is it about human beings that corresponds to the robust but elusive reality of the physical world? What are the 'moral facts' to which moral propositions are supposed to correspond if true and fail to correspond if false? They must be *general* aspects of human nature or of human life, if they are to have some claim to universality. It may be, however, that they are not stable in time. We must recognize both a strong and a weak universality thesis. A moral realist may have to countenance the possibility that human nature and human life have changed and may change again in ways relevant to those moral propositions we would take to be true and those we would take to be false; for instance a human race poised on the brink of extinction in the depths of an ice-age may be living a form of life that is in morally relevant ways different from the form of life of an over fecund culture, rich in resources.

Moral realism does not entail that there is only one set of moral facts, subserving human forms of life in all their historical and geographical diversity. We may hold to moral realism for each distinct human epoch, and so explain why there is moral diversity. Conceived on the model of scientific facts the epochal moral facts, applying to all human beings alive in that period, would be both foundational, the ultimate source of assessments of moral propositions in that historical time, and also objective, that is not brought into being by the making of moral judgements by this or that tribe or its shamans and moral entrepreneurs. But they would not be universal in the strong sense, that is the ultimate source of morality for all human societies at all times. With this caveat in mind, and reminding ourselves that we have found the idea of a foundation of morality in the facts of actual human preferences, we shall turn to examine some candidates for the role of 'moral fact'.

Needs   It seems hardly possible to deny that there are some universal human needs in the strong, pan-historical sense, and that all human forms of life must submit to them. The most incontrovertible are rooted in biology. But in addition to the needs for nourishment, shelter and so on, biologists have offered other needs that since they concern inter-animal relations come close to having the kind of moral force that we recognize as relevant to contemporary moralities. There seems to be a need to set up dominance hierarchies, to destroy the bearers of a rival's genes, and so on. It seems to us that these needs, though biologically universal, could hardly recommend themselves to morally sophisticated people. Indeed one might argue that morality is in place in human life just to discipline the thrust of biological imperatives.

Well-being   Since antiquity there has been frequent use of a notion of the good or best life. Ultimate moral assessments might be capable of being treated according to the principle of bivalence if set against this background. So the claim that it is *true* that one should help the needy is so judged with respect to the degree to which it subserves the realization of the best life. Several notorious questions surface at this point. Is there one and only one 'best life'? How is the best life to be identified? Welfarists see it in terms of the achievement and maintenance of certain psychological states, such as pleasure and intellectual satisfaction. Eudæmonists see it in terms of a way of living in which each human being is engaged in the deepest way, in particular with respect to the realization of his or her capacities or potentials. According to Aristotle it is a life in which virtue is expressed in action.[2] Of course as health freaks have pointed out there is a feeling of rightness and even ecstasy to be had as one lives the good life. But enjoying the effects of one's own endorphins cannot be definitive of the good life, only identificatory of it. So there is an aesthetic as well as a moral element in the actual realization of Aristotelian eudæmonia.

Neither of these aspects of moral realism is immune from serious objections or reservations. There are problems with the use of the criterion of bivalence to define moral realism via correspondence of moral judgements with moral facts, and problems with the idea of the virtuous life. The former runs into trouble in the many cases in which we want to use notions like degrees of truth, verisimilitude or some such, as any progressivist conception of either science or of the moral development of humankind is bound to require. It would be as extraordinary if we were in possession of a clear surview of the realists' moral universe as it would be if we were to claim to have such a view of the physical world. Like scientific realism, moral realism is wedded to the idea of moral progress, of getting a better idea of what the moral virtues are. This implies that we may have only a dim perception of moral truths, and that there are deeper moral insights to be achieved. What sort of insights would these be? There seems to be a closed pattern of circular reasoning here. The virtuous life is defined as that which enhances and protects personhood, while personhood is what the virtuous life defines and enhances. This circle accounts perhaps for the frequency with which eudæmonists, the advocates of the moral virtue that lies in living the most fulfilling life, have shifted in practice to aesthetic criteria to identify eudæmonist life ways.

Checked against our three distinguishing characteristics by which we assess the degree to which an anti-relativist doctrine is absolutist, moral realism is clearly objectivist. Whether a moral proposition is true or false, according to moral realists does not depend upon human opinion or state of belief, but only on the 'moral facts'. Consider the following argument:

I: 'Non-Caucasians do not feel pain as acutely as Caucasians'

II: 'It is wrong to torture people whether or not I is true and whether or not anyone believes it'.

The moral realist holds that propositions like II are true, that there are moral facts and they are just like proposition I, candidates for truth and falsity. Of course we hold that I is false!

Moral realism is foundationalist since for every tribe there are moral truths to which every rational member must agree, just as they must agree with ordinary matters of fact, and against which all moral judgements are to be assessed.

But as we have so far expounded moral realism it falls short of being universalist. Our Kantian criteria allow us to distinguish moralities from maxims of prudence. But none of the arguments for moral realism has succeeded in showing that what is objective and foundational for the morality of each tribe, *must* be the same for all tribes. It is logically possible that for different tribes there are different and distinct domains of moral facts. The moral realist has yet to establish that there is anything relevant to moral judgements that corresponds to the one material world that is considered to be relevant to the truth and falsity of scientific judgements by scientific realists. The step to

universalism will need to be supported by the identification of a common moral 'reality' to which the moral
intuitions of all the tribes of mankind can be submitted.

If the nature of moral judgements cannot be used to
discover the one true moral system, perhaps something
like human nature or the human form of life can provide
the transcendental roots of a universal and true morality.
This idea has had its most careful and most controversial
development in the long sequence of 'natural law' theories.

Natural law: universal imperatives[3]

There is, some hold, a natural law, applicable unequivocally to all human beings and which all human beings,
when it is brought to their notice, should acknowledge by
reason of their rational faculties, but which, as St Thomas
observed, not everyone will. Lloyd (1985) points out that
there are two ways in which we might try to arrive at a
formulation of a moral law applicable to and worthy to be
acknowledged by all human kind, a moral law to which
the law of the land must answer.

1   *The a posteriori anthropological argument*: All people at all
    times have acknowledged such and such an injunction
    or prohibition, so we conclude that people should
    continue to adhere to such injunctions and prohibi-
    tions. We might support this argument by returning to
    pick up one of the arguments of the Boasians, that the
    ubiquity of subscription to the principle in question
    showed that somehow it suited and facilitated human
    life. We think it would generally be conceded that this
    argument fails for the familiar Humean reason that it
    confuses prescriptive and descriptive discourse.

2   *The a priori teleological argument*: Human kind has a
    proper *telos* or end and a proper life form which would
    facilitate the realization of this end. Both the end and
    the proper form of life are to be discovered by reason.
    'The good of a species is the end it will reach if its
    progress is not impeded' (Lloyd, 1985: 94). As it stands
    this formulation lacks a clear specification of what sort
    of *telos* would secrete a moral law. Specifying the
    proper end of human kind is no easy task, as we shall
    see when we come to examine the attempts by Hart
    (1975) and Finnis (1980).

It is in various forms of the teleological argument that we
find the doctrine of natural law.

Prudential teleology   There is a version that we could call
'prudential teleology' based on what biology and anthropology can tell us of the proper state of human kind. Law
must have a minimum content based on the facts of
biology and psychology, that is it must reflect not just
which customs prevail, but also the very nature of humanity. From this standpoint a custom, however widespread,
could be criticized as against the best long term interest of
humankind. On this account natural law is a set of
principles 'to satisfy our needs and enhance our chances of
survival' (Hart, 1975 as quoted in Lloyd, 1985: 92). There
are some serious objections to this way of grounding the
case for natural law.
   Apart from the most primitive requirements for biological survival the needs of human beings are notoriously
unstable. If based on needs 'natural law' would be always
changing, contrary to one of the characteristics Aquinas
takes to be central to the notion. The problem is to see
how we could get any moral discrimination concerning

needs without turning to an independent moral criterion. For instance is there a need for unlimited human reproduction? This need seems to be obsolete now that advances in medicine and nutrition have meant that the tribe is not in danger of extinction. Rather the contrary. Nor can the moral force of natural law be derived from the prudential teleology of mere human survival. Why should there be any human beings at all? Perhaps the universe would be better, in some biological sense if there were none. Without them a greater diversity of species would survive. The human impact on the biosphere has been dramatic. Species are becoming extinct at an extraordinary rate largely due to direct and indirect human interference. The moral value of human existence cannot be found in biology.

These comments show that Hart's arguments lack a step, namely that which would make natural law not only prudent to implement but morally obligatory. One defence might be to deny that the category of moral obligatoriness applies to the law. According to the doctrine of positive law, legal ordinances are no more than ways of achieving practical orderliness, like traffic regulations. Law and morality would inhabit different spheres. Hart does not subscribe to such a radical reduction. For him the resolution of the problem is found in the opposite line of thought; that ultimately morality is a superior form of prudence.

Moral teleology   The full blown doctrine of natural law as a moral teleology that purports to establish a level of moral absolute found its most influential exponent in St Thomas Aquinas (1270 [1945]). The argument is to be found mostly in the *Summa Theologica* I–II, Questions XCI–XCIV. According to Thomas there are four kinds of law: eternal, natural, human and divine. It is in the interrelations between them that moral absolutes become incorporated in the heart of a morally informed law.

Eternal law 'is nothing else than the exemplar of divine wisdom, as directing all actions and movements' (Q. XCIII, Art. 1).

Natural law is defined in the *Summa Theologica* (hereafter ST) I–II, Question XCI, Art. 2 as follows: 'the rational creature . . . has a share of the eternal reason, whereby it has a natural inclination to its proper act or end; and this participation of the eternal law in the rational creature is called the natural law.' In Question XCIV, Art. 6 he adds a most important qualification: 'there belong to the natural law . . . certain most common precepts that are known to all . . . the natural law . . . cannot in any way be blotted out from men's hearts.' Natural law is known at the level of precepts and from these human law, the law of states and governments, is derived: 'from the precepts of the natural law . . . the human reason needs to proceed to the more particular determination of certain matters . . . these . . . are called human law' (Q. XCI, Art. 3).

Divine law is needed in addition to natural and human law because human beings do not have the competence to judge a variety of matters, such as private thoughts, the overall balance of good and evil and so on. But the heart of the argument for a moral absolute enshrined in natural law is the idea of participation of the eternal law in the natural and of the natural in the human. This descending chain is made possible by the common property of rationality that defines both God and his creatures.

Since '. . . the proper effect of law is to lead its subjects to their proper virtue' (Q. XVIV, Art. 4) the law must be '. . . allotted to him [humankind] according to his proper natural condition . . . [that is] he should act in accordance with reason' (Q. XCI, Art. 6). The law of each creature is allotted according to its proper nature, and thus must lead to virtue.

Is this a doctrine of moral absolutism? Thomas addresses that question in Q. XCIV, Art. 4, where he asks whether the natural law is the same for all human kind. He answers that . . . 'as regards common principles . . . truth or rectitude is the same for all, and is equally known by all . . .'. However, though the truth is known to all, the conclusions drawn from these precepts are neither known to all nor are they the same for all the possible conditions of human existence. We touch here on the distinction drawn in Roman jurisprudence between '*jus*', as in *jus gentium*, the law for all people, and *lex*, the law of some state, in the way that 'Thou shalt not kill' is realized locally as a law against murder in the furtherance of theft. In accordance with this distinction Aquinas defines 'law', the edicts of a properly constituted authority, as 'nothing else but a dictate of practical reason emanating from the ruler who governs a perfect community' (Q. XCI, Art. 1).

There are two levels of criticism that one might level at Aquinas' procedure for deriving 'natural law'.

1 The degree to which human law is 'natural' depends on the degree to which human law-makers can infallibly discern the precepts of eternal law as that law participates in natural law. That a precept is known to all must, in the Thomistic scheme be a necessary condition for its being part of natural law, but it clearly cannot be a sufficient condition. Everyone may share a precept that is anathema to God. Nor is our grasp of natural law a matter of making an inductive guess at what God is up to! Without an independent access to

eternal law there is no way in which genuine and bogus universal precepts could be assigned their rightful place in the moral order expressed in natural law. Indeed in insisting that there is a need for divine law as a supplement to natural law Thomas more or less concedes the limitation of human understanding in moral matters.

2 Aquinas introduces a distinction between just and unjust law that he needs since he has explained the obligatoriness of a human law by reference to the shared rationality of those subject to the law and of its authorized promulgator. But since there is no certainty that human beings or their institutions of government are actually rational what is to prevent an authority promulgating an unjust law which is enthusiastically received by an equally irrational populace? The distinction cannot be grounded in the procedure for deriving natural law, but must be added *ad hoc*.

It seems that the determining role that Thomas assigns to eternal law weakens the claim of any actual legal system to enshrine moral absolutes. Can rationality and human nature alone engender a natural law sufficiently robust to serve as a moral absolute? This project has been the aim of John Finnis (1980).

Finnis' argument is based on the assertion that 'normative conclusions of natural law are not based on observation of human or any other nature, but on a reflective grasp of what is self-evidently good for human beings'. Natural law is not revealed by an anthropological and historical survey of actual legal systems, but must be discovered *a priori*, by reflection on the conditions necessary for human flourishing and what will bring them about. There are many problems with this idea. Why should individuals deem themselves to be morally obliged to sustain the institutions that serve this end? Would it not simply be prudent to do so? How could we possibly obtain a reflective grasp of what is good for human beings if we have no recourse to knowledge of human or any other nature? Suppose I was under the impression that human beings only realized their full potential when in pain. It would then surely be proper for me to proclaim a sado-masochistic life form as 'good for human beings'? To rule out this reflective conclusion we must at least disagree with the impression, and that is to disagree on a matter of fact. As we shall see Finnis' own list of human goods are tied tightly to a rather narrow and parochial conception of human nature.

At the heart of Finnis' version of natural law theory is a radical individualism. The basic psychological 'good' is the ability to 'bring one's own intelligence to bear on choosing one's actions, one's style of life and in shaping one's own character'. This appears to some disadvantage when set in contrast to a view of life in which the basic psychological good would be the power to take a sympathetic attitude to the needs of others. Many would surely find Finnis' choice of basic psychological good morally offensive. It is important in assessing Finnis' scheme to keep in mind that his deep adherence to individualism is an ungrounded principle.

In applying the scheme to the problem of the sources of law Finnis recognizes two categories of law, focal and peripheral. Focal law consists of the rules, sanctions and judicative functions set down by established authority for the common good, and which are grounded in 'natural law'. Peripheral law consists of those regulations which are not so grounded, for example whether we parallel or diagonal park has little to do with human flourishing. How do we tie the notion of focal law as a set of regulations conducive to the common good to the basic psychological good, 'what is good for human beings', in such a way as to bring out something like a natural law foundation, while at the same time importing the necessary moral element that provides the normative force so far absent from the system? The common good is ensured by a kind of weak transcendental argument. It seems that Finnis wants to argue that there are certain characteristics of the good life, a life in which each individual flourishes in some manner that is characteristically human and which is defined ego-centrically, for the realization of which membership of a community is a necessary condition. Law sustains the community in which the Finnisian egoist can flourish. But natural law theory, of which Finnis' scheme is claimed to be an up to the minute version is universalist. It ties in to human nature in general. The universal element is provided by a kind of quasi-anthropological argument from an account of the seven basic features of the 'good life' as Finnis sees it. He holds that by direct intuition we can grasp that the following are the necessary components of human flourishing or at least a subset of these components: (i). life; (ii). knowledge; (iii). play; (iv). aesthetic experience; (v). sociability; (vi). practical reasonableness; and (vii). religion. Finnis asserts that 'all human beings strive for these things'. At first sight this remark seems inconsistent with his rejection of observations of human nature as grounds for the choice of seven goods. But that would be to misunderstand his position. Our reasons for accepting these goods are not empirical, but intuitive, in that he believes that we can directly grasp that these are the goods the realization of which will bring about human flourishing.

There are three elements in his position:

1　An *a priori* assertion that there are basic human goods, the Finnisian septet, that conduce to a flourishing life.
2　A claim that the seven components of the good life are known intuitively and have no need of anthropological support.
3　An analytical argument that is intended to show that the existence of an orderly community is a necessary condition for the realization of the flourishing life adumbrated in (2).

The final conclusion is that there is a 'Natural Law', that is there are edicts which make possible an orderly community in which Finnisian egocentric actors can flourish, getting in a few sets of tennis with their friends after mass. When we instantiate such vague concepts as 'game' and 'religion' that characterize the flourishing Finnisian their derivative and even trivial character becomes clear. Since only just laws can emerge from the above three elements, the contrast between focal and penumbral law guarantees that in the process of legal criticism the moral and the truly legal coincide. The *moral* foundation of Finnisian natural law theory is the claim in (2) above. It is also the key step in achieving the universal span that natural law theory requires.

As an absolutist or anti-relativist morality Finnis' position hangs on (2). Let us look at his seven desiderata, and subject them to the 'intuitive grasp'. Remember that the test must show not only that people do flourish when these goods are realized but that they should. It is the rationality of human beings that links the basic intuitions to the flourishing life, to life, knowledge, play, aesthetic experience, sociability, practical reasonableness and religion. None of the seven 'goods' seems to be definitive of a flourishing form of life to which we must give our *moral* allegiance. Notoriously knowledge unqualified by moral sensibility in its development and application is as often a bar to human flourishing as it is a ground for it. One of us has no use for play in a flourishing life. Are the Desert Fathers to be found violating Natural Law in their self-imposed isolation? Can the genuinely agnostic not flourish? To make any of these a morally summoning state of being some moral principles other than these are surely required. If it is argued that advancing one of these as a reason for an action is what makes that reason a good reason, we can cite the same range of objections as we have already listed for rejecting the claim of infallible intuitions in favour of these as goods. Only if there is such a ground could these seven desiderata be the foundation of a morality of law. Only then could Finnisian Natural Law theory be seen as a form of moral realism.

It seems to us that the only way the list of seven goods could be germane to the question of moral realism is if it could be shown to incorporate conditions necessary and sufficient for there to be a community of persons, sustained in being by the practices which would realize the above list of goods. But that is to change the basis of the argument from a claim about matters of fact to a philosophical analysis which would be part of a transcendental argument, of a Kantian sort. The moral absolutist can find no comfort in Finnis' account of the moral basis of law. It is either disguised anthropology and so lacks an *a priori* guarantee of universality, or it rests on intuitions which lacking a foundation seem to be arbitrary. As it is presented it is immune from comment since anyone who offered an example of a tribe which seemed to flourish while pursuing other goods than Finnis intuits, for

instance Calvinists and other gloomy Protestants, is ruled
out of play.

Moral realism and the coherence of a form of life   We turned to
natural law theory in the hope of finding a source of
universal, objective and foundational moral truth through
the ideas of an 'external' referent for moral intuitions. The
analogy with scientific realism proved unconvincing.
Neither the Eternal Law of Thomas Aquinas nor Finnis'
intuitions about the necessary constituents of a flourishing
life were convincing either. Before abandoning moral
realism altogether let us see if there is another way with
truth. The general idea, proposed with a wealth of detail,
by Brink (1989), is that the 'external' reference, so to say,
of moral propositions, through which their objective
justification is to be sought, is a totalized system of beliefs.
Moral beliefs are supposed to find places within this
system. They are true or false just in so far as they fit or do
not fit within such a system of beliefs. 'Fit' must be
something like 'be logically coherent with'. Is there a
coherentist argument that yet manages to skirt the objection that there could be and indeed that there actually are
different and independent totalized systems of belief? At
first sight it would seem that no coherentist account of
belief, be it moral or physical, could be absolutist, that is
either universal, foundational or objective. This might be
because a plethora of independent, totalized systems of
belief are possible for any universe. Or it might be, Berlin
has argued (Gray, 1994) that there are no internally
coherent systems of belief in the moral or political sphere.
It has long been a standard objection to the coherence
theory of truth – to the idea that we should accept or reject
propositions on the grounds of their degree of coherence

with some totalized systems of beliefs – cannot give one any reason to support a claim that that proposition is true, since there are, in principle, indefinitely many alternative totalized systems of propositions that are internally coherent but with which this proposition does not agree. Adopting coherence as one's favoured account of truth seems to lead straight to relativism. There is only one world, but innumerable systems of propositions.

At this point we return to the writings of Brink (1989: 125–135), who has presented a kind of modulation of the recent attempts in philosophy of science to have a coherentist realism. Brink draws on the neo-idealist philosophers, especially Blanshard (1939), for the materials to construct an argument to rebut the obvious objection sketched above. A totalized belief system includes not only first-order beliefs about this or that subject matter, but second-order beliefs about those first-order beliefs. A scientific belief system includes beliefs about the reliability of first-order scientific beliefs. For example we might believe that one's belief that sodium reacts spontaneously with water at room temperature is well founded. But these cannot be about the reliability of first order beliefs as representations of an independent reality since even if it existed we have no access to it. Blanshard argued that the coherence theory of truth is only 'objective' in so far as one can treat the world as of the same 'stuff' as thought, that as potentially logically related to belief. For example rules and actions are of the same 'stuff'. As Wittgenstein put it: 'An expectation and its fulfilment meet in language'. The appropriate second order beliefs would be beliefs with regard to the efficacy of first-order beliefs as guides to action. Complicated inductive arguments based on this way of combining coherence and realism have already been sketched in chapter 3. For a defence of moral realism along coherentist lines one would need to construct an analogue of this layered structure of beliefs that takes moral beliefs as first-order judgements. One can believe that one's belief that racial discrimination is wrong is well founded, or if shared would lead to human emancipation, and believe at a yet higher order that human emancipation is also a good. Just as second-order beliefs in the totalized system of scientific beliefs are beliefs about how first-order beliefs fare in helping us to manage the material world, so second-order beliefs in the totalized system of beliefs about human nature and human life-forms would be beliefs about how first-order beliefs fare in helping us to manage the human world, for example to what degree they are efficacious in promoting human welfare.

But this argument seems to be no advance on the arguments we have already examined in this chapter. All we can say is that a moral belief is to be incorporated coherently into our totalized system of belief if it subserves our conception of human needs, aims, ends and goods. This argument does nothing to show that there may not be any number of forms of life for which human beings might be successfully trained, where first-order beliefs differ radically one from another, though each, in context, is efficacious. Beating children may lead to happy adults in one culture and to neuroses in another. Second-order beliefs which are about the efficacy of first-order beliefs must be exactly as culturally diverse as are systems of first-order beliefs. Local beliefs about what is good and bad, about what practices would subserve the preservation, flourishing and development of each tribal form of life, and even of an Evil Empire, need not, so far as we can see, necessarily converge on a single, coherent form of life.

Are there moral systems?

We owe the idea of a somewhat different approach to the questions we are addressing in this chapter, to Bernard Harrison (1985). He has pointed out to us how much our own and others' ways of formulating moral relativism, depend on the idea of a 'system of values'. It is to such systems, if there are any, that moral principles are relative. It is such systems which, it is presumed, are so culturally and historically diverse, as to offer no chance of a settled foundation for morality. But what if there are no such systems? What if the very idea of a moral system is a typical philosopher's over-rationalization of a roughly aggregated, somewhat inconsistent bouquet of principles, maxims and values, that never do cohere in the way that the use of the word 'system' would imply, as Berlin has argued (Gray, 1994)? Coherence of moral systems must be a necessary condition of relativism since to show that a moral principle is relative to a system we would need to show both that it can be derived from that system, and that the principles, definitions etc. in the system should be related in some way. In case a principle is inconsistent with the relevant system then it is not a moral principle and so does not come up for consideration in respect of moral relativism.

If moral orders are not systems in the required sense, moral relativism would reduce to the trivial observation that within a broad base of generic moral principles people differ as to how to treat particular cases in which some generic moral value is instantiated. For instance cruelty to children is acceptable in some societies since it is their way of ensuring the ultimate good of the child, and discharging their responsibilities to it. We may be morally relativist about 'Spare the rod and spoil the child' while being morally absolutist about the duty parents have to ensure the welfare of their offspring. In one society the conflict between moral abhorrence of cruelty and moral commitment to care is resolved in favour of the latter, in others it may be resolved in favour of the former. Both societies share both moral principles, but resolve conflicts in locally differing ways.

It seems to us that Harrison's observations are just. Yet what do they bear against? It must surely be against the anthropological argument that differing moral judgements in different societies and at different times refute the thesis that there are transcultural and pantemporal moral principles. If moral judgements differ because they represent differing local compromises, they cannot be offered as evidence for a *modus tollens* like argument that a certain moral principle adhered to by Tribe A is not mandatory for Tribe B. Yet these local compromises are the very stuff of life and, we presume from Harrison's citation of cruel customs amongst traditional Chinese, a matter of regularity. It is not that there is no moral relativism. Rather moral judgements are culture relative at some intermediate level between the highest moral principles and mere casuistry. In short the anthropological argument does not demonstrate that there are no universal moral principles.

There are no objective moral facts, if we follow Harrison. He makes a good case for holding that every actual moral judgement must represent some sort of compromise between locally valid but non-cohering principles, none of which reflect any extra-cultural reality. Yet, there may still be moral universals, intuitions that are held as widely as humankind. At the same time we may still find a foundation for morality in the conditions for the moral protection of persons while acknowledging that these conditions are not objective, that is have no moral value outside a human context.

NOTES

1   It has been argued, for example by Harrison (1985), that the version of the categorical imperative we have set down as (i) above is less subtle than the original Kantian principle. Kant distinguishes perfect from imperfect duties. Two people may each see themselves as having a duty that they do not see as a duty for the other, while conforming to the principle that whatever one wills for others one must will for oneself. What is universal is the principle that one has a duty as a rational will to what one conceives to be one's duty, whatever that might be.

2   In the Eudæmian ethics Aristotle sees virtue stemming from the life of a collective, while in the Nichomachean ethics it is individual virtues of the fully developed human potential that are the grounds of morality. As Kenny argues (1992) it would be a mistake to take these doctrines to be in radical conflict.

3   R. Harré owes a great deal of his understanding of natural law theory to a course of lectures given by Abisi Sharakya at Binghamton University in 1991. They were a model of clarity and careful analysis. This chapter has also benefited from generous critical feedback from Dan Robinson.

6

From Relativism to Anarchy

Introduction

Our analysis has been based on two, taken-for-granted
oppositions. On the one hand there is the opposition
between nature and culture, realized, for example, in the
opposition between material nature and the discourses and
models of the natural sciences. On the other hand, there is
the opposition between one aspect or part of culture and
another, for example between a working political constitution and the discourses of political philosophy and
history; or at a lesser level the opposition between a
working constitution and the popular discourses of the
day. Human affairs and the grammatical conventions and
semantic repertoires of the discourses which address those
affairs are notoriously in flux. But the world, which taken
as an ever-changing array of particulars is also in flux, can
be shown to be rooted in a multiple hierarchy of types, the
ultimate types of beings are not in flux. This was the
greatest insight of antiquity, reflected in the famous slogan
that defined the task of science as the saving of the
appearances, that as the revealing the universality and

stability that lies behind, and in the end accounts for the diversity with which we are ordinarily presented.

The strongest varieties of relativism involve the rejection all three absolutisms; universalism, objectivism, and foundationalism. The three most notorious are based upon a projection of the considerations that speak in favour of the varieties of relativism which characterize the reflective relations that a culture bears to itself, onto the relations that cultures bear to the one and only world of material nature. We have already seen how Bohr's philosophy of science enables us to do justice to the insight that concepts and instruments influence which aspect of material nature we can force to reveal itself in the affordances of experimental and observational set ups. Undermining that resolution are the claims for strong relativism put forward by Rorty, Feyerabend and Gergen. In each case we shall show how their claims collapse once the slide from the culture/culture relation to the culture/nature relation is revealed. We shall call the strong relativist position in which all three aspects of absolutism are rejected, 'philosophical anarchism'.

The Extremists: From Relativism to Anarchism

Each of our exemplary philosophical anarchists seems to have picked on a different variety of relativism from which to launch their preemptive strikes upon the universe of meaning, knowledge and value. Rorty (1980, 1989) has developed an anarchistic anti-foundationalism; Feyerabend (1975) has developed an anarchistic anti-universalism, and Gergen (1991) has developed an anarchistic anti-objectivism. It is important for us to counter these extremist developments, since they bring defensible relativist positions into disrepute. It is our contention that a wide variety of combinations of assertions and denials of the three absolutist positions make sense. Though none has unqualified support cases can be made out for most of these combinations of assertion and denial except that which jointly denies all three aspects of absolutism in all contexts. Characteristic of the writings of each author is a 'slide into anarchy', a fallacious pattern of reasoning which we have called the 'family resemblance fallacy', after Wittgenstein's felicitous phrase. Wittgenstein (1953) pointed out that many a common term is used in a range of subtly different ways. There is no essence common to all the entities, types, processes and so on that make up the whole range of its application. The word 'rule', for example, has a huge range of uses and there is no one feature that is common to all the edicts, instructions, conventions, orders and so on that are from time to time called 'rules'. Such ranges of uses almost always constitute a field of family resemblances, rather than a group of hidden commonalities. While there are similarities between many of the ways in which a word is used, there may be some which, though linked by a range of inter-mediate cases, are nevertheless quite dissimilar. Assuming that there must be a common essence because just one word is used, tempts one to pick on one use and to treat all others as subtle variants on it, encouraging one to see identities where there are merely a pattern of likenesses and differences. Widely separated members of a family of uses may have nothing in common. To slip into this assumption of a common essence is to commit the 'family resemblance fallacy'. It is almost always a mistake to export the principles of 'grammar' governing the use of a word in one part of a domain, to another part of that domain. In each case the arguments of our anarchists exhibit the family resemblance fallacy. In particular they fail to preserve radical differences between the inter-cultural domains of discourse as adjusted to artifacts, and extra-cultural discourse where theories confront, albeit indirectly, an intransigent material world.

Feyerabend: Beyond logic and truth

We share Feyerabend's (1975) doubts about the values or virtues of logicism. The idea that the major features of the way we make sense of our environment and of ourselves are to be explicated and their normative power explained by extricating the logical 'core' of our cognitive activities has had a pernicious effect on philosophy of science. It has left the amazing powers of natural science quite unexplic-ated and worse, has led some to deny them altogether. If logic does not reign then what remains must be irrational and, in the end, anarchic. It is to this proposition that Feyerabend's studies of the history of science are intended to point. Here is another slide, based on a failure to grasp that there is more than one alternative to logicism as an account of science, and that the demonstration of the inadequacy of logicism does not establish the anarchistic interpretation of science.

   Feyerabend's anarchistic view of method is based upon an ironic reversal of the logicist, and particularly of the Popperian version of the logicist conception of methodo-logy. If you want a formula, like Popper's 'conjectures and refutations', that will capture the essence of scientific method, says Feyerabend, then the best candidate would be 'anything goes'. Of course Feyerabend is far from thinking that anything will do as an answer to a scientific question provided it is pushed by a persuasive enough person. His problem is to fill the gap between the evident shortfall in what would officially count as evidence for a novel point of view (or paradigm in Kuhn's Fleckian terminology) and the rapidity with such new points of view are actually taken up, not just as innovations but as orthodoxies.

Feyerabend's relativism is concerned with what is to count as a significant observation in the considerations that weigh with working scientists. There is, he believes, a tight conceptual circle between the theory one espouses and the choice of significant observations that are taken to support the theory. An observation, say that a horseman can catch the spear he throws up at full gallop, takes its significance from a theory. This phenomenon is significant just in so far as it is illustrative of the principle of linear momentum. It is not that it serves as a Popperian refutation of the Aristotelian principle of the natural decay of motion. A determined advocate of mechanical peristalsis could have made the horseman's spear conform to Aristotelian physics. In his studies of the 'scientific revolution' Feyerabend (1975) concentrates on Galileo's works, especially his use of the telescope. Neither Copernican nor Ptolemaic astronomy could survive the refutatory force of the available evidence, so in a sense both are Popper-wise refuted. But in his advocacy of Copernicus 'Galileo prevails because of his style and his clever techniques of persuasion'. 'Factuality', 'what is natural [and so taken for granted]', and every other feature of the components of the traditional inductivist, hypothetico–deductivist or fallibilist methodologies, are only relative to a certain point of view. As such they support that point of view, which was not arrived at by courtesy of the role these 'components' played in some logical schema.

Various important conclusions follow for Feyerabend
from these and other observations about the practice
of science. Particularly important, in this context, is the
cognitive/linguistic phenomenon of *incommensurability*.
The idea of the possible incommensurability of ways of
thinking about the world has its source in certain features
of language use. Feyerabend took his arguments from
Whorf (1956), particularly the thesis that languages 'secrete' cosmologies. These are incorporated in covert classifications, bringing about 'patterned resistances to widely
divergent points of view', preventing anyone realizing
that an alternative to the prevailing orthodoxy has been
presented. If two languages are such that they 'secrete'
incompatible cosmologies, then, says Feyerabend, we
have incommensurability between the views of the world
each enables its users to formulate. Just the same features,
he asserts, as mark incommensurabilities of language can
be found in successive scientific theories. Unfortunately
Feyerabend offers no further examples from the sciences,
but turns to changes in artistic traditions and styles to
illustrate his thesis, a move we are now becoming familiar
with in anarchist authors.

In some general remarks on the application of these
ideas to science Feyerabend comes to the key consideration: a holistic theory of language. When a new term is
inserted into an old language it does not leave the language
unchanged. At just this point we have the beginning of the
slide from relativism into anarchy. According to Feyerabend (1975: 266) if there are two languages A and B, each
appropriate to its proper cosmos, we might try to express
the transition from the old A-view to a new B-view in the
following way: by adding the 'missing [B] terms to
language A, the missing [B] structures to the perceptual
world of A, and you [would] obtain cosmos B language

B, perception B,' But this would not work, says Feyer-abend. 'Neither commonsense terms, nor philosophical theories; neither painting and statuary, nor artistic concep-tions; neither religion, nor theoretical speculation contain a single element of A once a transition to B has been completed'. Why? Because, says Feyerabend, 'the "nature" of an object (= aggregate) in A is determined by the elements of the aggregate and the relation between the elements. . . . the elements and the relation *constitute* the object. When they are given the object is given as well. An addition does not *add* to cosmos A, it *undercuts* the principles that are needed in the construction of A-type [objects].' 'An entire world view, an entire universe of thought, speech, perception is dissolved' (op. cit. 266–67). Here is the transition from relativism to anarchy. If the dissolution is as wholesale and as deep as Feyerabend declares it to be, then no one living within the cosmos B can ever have any inkling whatever as to what it was like to inhabit cosmos A.

Ever since Feyerabend enunciated this thesis historians have offered a stream of counter examples (Papineau, 1979). The slide from some cases of mutual unintelligibil-ity to the claim that all cases of linguistic difference generate unintelligibility is obviously fallacious. This is not only because there are many examples of piecemeal changes in the rules for the use of a terminology, but also because Feyerabendian anarchism is paradoxical. In order to realize that one had witnessed a paradigm change one would need to have at least some inkling of the original meaning of the terms, say 'mass', 'time interval' etc. in the old paradigm. Otherwise it would be impossible to discern that these terms had now changed their meaning. There is indeed a relation between our choice of language and what we can pick out from the natural world. But it does not follow that what we pick out is a language-induced artefact. Nor does it follow that we are precluded from understanding how the world appeals or appears to the users of different languages.

Gergen: Beyond authenticity and responsibility

Our second exemplar of the slide from relativism to anarchy is K. J. Gergen's *The Saturated Self* (Gergen, 1991). This text illustrates a different range of fallacious reasonings from our previous example. Where Feyerabend fails to grasp that there are many small semantic steps from the lexicon of one paradigm to another, Gergen's study exemplifies a persistent failure to keep track of crucial distinctions among the specific forms that generic concepts may take. In the very first chapter we are warned of the continuing 'erosion of the self'. But in that chapter in the course a couple of pages (op. cit. : 4–5) five different notions of 'self' are on parade. First of all there is this: 'our characterizations of self – the ways we make ourselves intelligible to others'. Then there is 'selves as possessors of real and identifiable characteristics', and the 'sets of charac-teristics attributed to individual selves'. If, as Gergen says, such sets have changed, this presupposes that there is some use for the concept of 'individual self' without which the very idea of changing characteristics makes no sense. Then there is the 'single, autonomous individual' with capacities for self-direction and responsibility. We are also offered 'personality' as another synonym for self. In discussing Geertz's (1973) classic work on the psychology of the Balinese, 'self' seems to be taken to be the same as 'person'. In sum Gergen elides two ontologically utterly different notions; the set of attributes that can be ascribed to a subject, and the subject to which they are ascribed. In the terminology of logic he elides qualitative identity with numerical identity.

As far as we can see none of the many cases and examples he offers suggests for one moment that selves, in the sense of that which is numerically identical as a person, the one they are, is threatened or eroded or in any way compromised by the fact that we must adapt to many diverse contexts in our everyday lives. Everything he cites tends to show that it is not true that a person is qualitatively identical across situations and across times. Well, we knew that! The important point that Gergen does make is that qualitative identities of persons are constituted relative to languages and cultures. He says nothing to suggest that numerical identities may be constructions too. That is the thesis of the Vygotskians (Harré, 1983; Wertsch, 1985), a thesis about the origins of the self in psychological symbiosis with others and of the nature of the self as the sense of one's numerical identity as an individual person, a thesis to which it is astounding that Gergen pays no attention. Nevertheless, without any argumentative preliminaries, he announces on p. 242 that 'without coordinate acts of communication, there is simply no "I" to be articulated'.

Throughout the book there seems to be a suggestion that postmodern selves, individual human beings suffering neither from amnesia nor senile dementia, and so knowing who they are, may take on simultaneously and from time to time different personal attributes. Persons, conceived this way, Gergen suggests, may somehow be less constrained by the 'romantic' notion of authenticity and the modernist notion of personal responsibility. Of course this loosing of the bonds of morality does not follow from the perception of the variability of personal attributes at all. Gergen's argument is based on the role of languages (sometimes Gergen writes inconsistently about 'the language') in inculcating or bringing into being diverse catalogues of attributes in those who acquire them. But that invites us to consider the necessary conditions for anyone to be able to acquire and use a language in the first place. In declaring that 'If we give postmodern discourse an opportunity to expand, to make use of the available resources of the language. . .' we shall be free of the moral constraints of personal responsibility, Gergen quite omits to consider whether there may be necessary conditions for the possibility of language as a human practice, that undermine the alleged moral openness of the postmodern condition.

Holiday (1988) has made a strong case for the general thesis that amongst the necessary conditions for the possibility of the use of language for its everyday purposes, there are certain moral universals to which a language community must subscribe. As he puts it, in Wittgensteinian terms, there are certain language games which must have a place in the form of life of any community of language users. His candidate language-games for this role are built around the general requirement that there be interpersonal trust, a certain kind of attitude of respect that speakers and hearers must have to one another, that a conversation be possible. There must also be a 'reverence for ritual'. All that holds a language community together is a willingness to subscribe to rules of linguistic conduct that have no other sanction than that they are the conventions of the community.

A key argument, common to many ways of advocating 'gergenism', is based upon the idea that there are viable societies in which the tightly centred personhood of 'western' (and by that is usually meant 'middle-class American') individualism, is not to be found or is not the dominant mode of self-understanding. It is said that people in these other cultures do not see themselves as autonomous individuals but only as members of groups, families, clans, nations and so on. Yet this is sloppy anthropology. The difference in the cultural forms is there right enough, but its psychological groundings are not as they are presumed to be. It is not that the members of these cultures lack a sense of personal power and individual responsibility. Rather it is exercised reflexively, on those impulses and projects, intentions and putative actions, that if indulged in would disrupt the community. It is the general failure of postmodernism to take seriously the idea that there is a private as well as a public discourse that perhaps leads to this serious omission. Cultures differ in the way that agency and responsibility *concepts* figure in private and public discourses, not in the degree to which any human being is possessed of these concepts. As the comparative study of indexicality of pronoun systems shows every language has a way of indexing personhood with the unique and only body in which that person is embodied. Personal identity, in the sense of numerical oneness, is a universal feature of the sense of selfhood in all human societies. While something in human nature is culture-relative, something is not. Once again we reach the conclusion that coarse-grained general questions like 'Is human nature absolute or relative to culture?' fail to do justice to the complexity of the situations they invite us to consider.

Rorty: Beyond grounding and certainty

Rorty's anarchist theses are supported by two related but independent lines of argument. In his earlier work (Rorty,

1980) he developed a historically grounded critical analysis
of the invention of 'epistemology' as the study of the
foundations of knowledge. In his more recent work
(Rorty, 1989) his argument has shifted to an attempt to
find support for a pair of theses about 'truth' and the
nature of language. The final conclusion of the two works
is the claim that we human beings, living forever within
language, can assess the discourses of this or that cultural
group, including natural scientists, only by reference to
matters of practical convenience. Rorty expresses his
approval of the anarchistic attack on what he sees as the
absolutist pretensions of science in the following passage:

> great scientists invent descriptions of the world which are
> useful for the purposes of predicting and controlling what
> happens, just as poets and political thinkers invent other
> descriptions for other purposes. But there is no sense in
> which any of these descriptions is an accurate representa-
> tion of the way the world is in itself (Rorty, 1989: 4).

Running through both Rorty's works there is a tendency
to import as methods and criteria of assessment of the
knowledge engendering powers of the sciences, observations, insights and principles we quite properly use in
discussing the nature and quality of works of art, social
formations and other cultural artifacts. The assimilation of
the sciences to world relation to the cultural discourse to
artefact relation is characteristic of the post-modernist
analysis of modernism. But it violates one of Wittgenstein's deepest insights, that one must never take a family
resemblance to be an identity. Rorty's argument is an
outstanding example of the 'family resemblance fallacy'.
There is at most a family resemblance between the notions
of 'knowledge', 'enquiry', 'truth' and so on as used in
discussions of the works of human kind, including that

most elaborate and diverse of human artifacts the person, and the way these words are used in discussions of the 'works' of nature[1]. Rorty simply asserts, without argument, that we must agree that scientific revolutions are ' "metaphoric redescriptions" of nature rather than insights into the intrinsic nature of nature.' How his assertion is to be reconciled with such episodes as the discovery of the circulation of the blood, of the sexuality of flowering plants, or with the ionic account of the chemistry of solutions, with plate tectonics and so on is to say the least problematic. He offers no concrete examples to illustrate his contention.

Rorty's (1980) anti-foundationalist argument is based on a contrast between

> knowledge as a relation to propositions and thus . . . justification as relations between the proposition in question and other propositions . . . Or we may think of both knowledge and justification as privileged relations to the objects those propositions are about. If we think the first way, we will see no need to end the potentially infinite degrees of [justificatory propositions]. If we think in the second way we will want to get behind reasons to causes, beyond argument to compulsion from the object known. . . To reach that point is to reach the foundations of knowledge (op. cit.: 159).

Is knowledge created by relating one proposition to another, or by relating a proposition to its subject matter? If, as tradition had it, it is the latter, according to Rorty we must try to find out how an object of knowledge causes that knowledge in a human mind. In practice, impelled by this vision, we seek in the mind that mirrors nature 'a special privileged class of representations so compelling that their accuracy cannot be doubted. These privileged foundations will be the foundation of knowledge.' Various philosophers have offered somewhat similar candidates for this class of representations. There have been Lockean simple ideas, Humean impressions and Russellian sense-data. According to Rorty and we do not wish to deny this, there are no privileged representations. But to deny that there are foundations for knowledge is not to establish that a progressivist, world driven conception of the improvement of knowledge is not viable.

The key argument of the second phase of the slide from relativism to anarchy is again set within a historical framework: The German idealists, having achieved the great insight that 'the world of empirical science is a made world', nevertheless fell into the error of 'seeing mind, spirit, the depths of the human self, as having an intrinsic nature . . .' But, says Rorty, 'what was needed . . . was a repudiation of the very idea of anything . . . having an intrinsic nature to be expressed or represented.' But this claim is in need of argumentative support. It is the key to Rorty's anarchism.

> We need to make a distinction between the claim that the world is out there, and the claim that truth is out there. . . . most things in space and time are the effects of causes which do not include human mental states. To say that truth is not out there is simply to say that where there are not sentences, there is no truth, that sentences are elements of human languages and that human languages are human creations (Rorty, 1989: 4–5)

This banal observation is made telling by Rorty's claim that there are no facts in the world. 'Facts', for him, are 'sentence-shaped things', a charming if shallow metaphor. One might be tempted to think that the world helps us to decide between say, 'Strychnine is poisonous' and 'Strychnine is nourishing'. Rorty makes a distinction between the claim that the world contains the causes of our being justified in believing something and the claim that the world contains something which makes a sentence true. He thinks we can rid ourselves of the states of the world as truth-makers by attending to the holistic character of language. It is in spelling this out that Rorty makes the most startling assimilation of characteristics of political and artistic discourse to those of scientific. Of course the world doesn't make Jefferson's political vocabulary better than Aristotle's. But it does not follow that it is not the world that makes what Rorty is pleased to call Newton's 'jargon' better that Aristotle's, for discussing the laws of free fall, for instance.

Behind the assimilation of natural science to political philosophy lies a once common but grossly misleading reading of Wittgenstein's thesis that grammar is autonomous. Wittgenstein pointed out that we are free to chose whatever conventions of discourse we like. The world cannot constrain our choice of grammar. We could chose to say that a surface can be red and green all over at once. But, despite the occasional appearance of shot silk and purplish brown surfaces in our milieu, it is much more 'cost effective', to make it a rule of 'grammar' that the words 'red' and 'green' should be used in this disjunctive way. Wittgenstein adds, most tellingly, that to achieve a common life form we must not only agree in our linguistic conventions but also in practical judgements. Some grammars are better suited to the telling of coherent stories about the way the world is, and devising action guiding programmes that fit the world better than others, with respect to some standard we have set ourselves.

Again the assimilation of natural sciences to psychology and other human centred discourses is evident when Rorty once more writes of essences: 'the temptation to look for criteria [for deciding whether one 'grammar' is more revealing of reality than another] is a species of the more general temptation to think of the world, or the human self, as possessing an intrinsic nature, an essence' (Rorty, 1989: 6). While everything we now know about the discursive origins of the many diverse senses of self to be found among human beings points to the truth of the observation that there is no essential human nature, everything we now know about the development of the sciences points to the correctness of a properly circumscribed essentialism in physics. The real essence of hydrogen is the having of an atomic architecture consisting of a proton/electron pair. Atoms which do not have this architecture, for instance those which incorporate one or more neutrons in the nucleus are called respectively 'deuterium' and 'tritium'.

Rorty's misreading of Wittgenstein goes further. He couples it with an approving stance to some of the more tendentious views of Davidson about the nature of language. Language, so declares Rorty, is not to be thought of as a medium for representing how things are (with me, with you or with the natural world), but a more or less efficient tool for predicting what is likely to be said, done or to happen under this or that circumstance. A primitive positivism is fathered on Wittgenstein's subtle analysis. 'This Wittgensteinian attitude [sic], developed by Ryle and Dennett for minds and by Davidson for languages, naturalizes mind and language by making all questions about the relation of either to the rest of the universe causal questions, as opposed to questions about adequacy of representation or expression' (Rorty, 1989: 15). Quite apart from the decline of post-modernism into positivism which this passage so strikingly illustrates, it celebrates the erosion of the very idea of standards of correctness, of the normativity which is so characteristic of human affairs. Here the anarchistic side of post-modern permissiveness shows itself most clearly. Right and wrong opinions about states of the world are equally caused by the world. A proposal of marriage and a vicious rape may be equally caused by the attractions one human being exercises on another. According to Rorty the history of culture has no *telos*, such as the emancipation of humanity. Our culture, so he says, is something 'that took shape as a result of a great number of sheer contingencies'. If that were so how can we adjudicate between the two effects equally caused, between the marriage and the rape? This is surely a *reductio ad absurdum* of the post-modern stance to morality.

Finally it is worth reiterating that the most recent discussions of realism as a characterisation of the project of the physical sciences makes no use of the naive idea of a correspondence between statements and facts, between something linguistic and something non-linguistic (Aronson, Harré and Way, 1994). In our view the only way that anything linguistic could be *directly* related to anything material is as rules or prescriptions or plans for the construction of something material. On this view laws of nature (built up into theories) are functionally just such rules and prescriptions. They are rules for construction of models, virtual worlds that are our human surrogates for the real world to which we have only indirect access. But once we have built such a virtual world, in the laboratory or in the imagination or on paper, since it is thing-like we can compare it with the world, which is also thing-like in those aspects to which we can have perceptual access. Comparisons, under some constraint of relevance, enable us to say how well our virtual world has mapped the real world. Different constraints on relevance, different assessments of adequacy of mapping, constrain each domain of knowledge, but in each there are working criteria for judging whether a mapping is more or less adequate for the job in hand. The slippage from a constructionist account of the human world to a constructionist/positivist account of the physical world is blocked the moment we begin to pay close attention to how knowledge is arrived at through the use of the techniques of the physical sciences. We can leave the logicist myths behind us without adopting post-modernist anarchism.

In all three examples of relativism as anarchy, the strong relativism that denies that there is anything universal, objective or foundational in the content of cultures, we have detected the same fallacy. What is true of intercultural cognitive relationships is not true of all aspects of the relationships between cultures and the world they make available to us.

The project of defining and defending a relativism so radical that it rejects all three of the root ideas that define strong absolutism, at least as it is realized in the writings of our exemplars, Feyerabend, Gergen and Rorty must be adjudged a failure.

NOTES

1 One of the curiosities of Rorty's writings is his total neglect of the 'alternative' tradition in psychology, where the constructivist or discursive turn uproots naive scientism, and celebrates cultural diversity without sliding into post-modernism, and the abandonment of normativity (Harré and Gillett, 1994).

7

Residues and Resolutions

Introduction

In our discussion of arguments for and against relativisms and absolutisms: namely, universalism, objectivism and foundationalism, we have shown how different arguments highlight different patterns of relativist and anti-relativist positions. For example in some contexts one can be a universalist without being an objectivist or a foundationalist. All in all there are a variety of relativisms and absolutisms, each variety based on different patterns of ways in which one or more of the three root ideas in absolutism is denied.

We can set out the varieties of absolutism and relativism in the following table:

Strong absolutism (or Dogmatism):
Universalism with Objectivism and Foundationalism
Moderate absolutisms:
Universalism with Objectivism but without Foundationalism
Universalism with Foundationalism but without Objectivism
Moderate relativisms:
Anti-universalism with Objectivism but without Foundationalism

Anti-universalism with Foundationalism but without
Objectivism
Strong relativism (or Anarchism):
Anti-universalism with anti-Objectivism and anti-
Foundationalism

From the point of view of the controversies we have
examined the most important characteristic of systems of
meaning, of scientific theories, of ontologies and of moralities is their degree of universality of application. Whether
there is a basic vocabulary, a growing set of elementary
scientific facts, a basic set of ontological categories and a
root morality is often a local question, independent of
whether the meanings, theories, existents and moral
virtues are universal or not. Universalism need not be
coupled with foundationalism. Whether meanings are
given by denoting language-independent objects, whether
science is based on phenomena which are independent of
observers and their classificatory categories, and experimenters and their equipment, whether there is a world
which exists independently of any of our ways of observing and manipulating it, and whether there are moral
values independent of the lives and projects of those who
live them, are important issues. While the choice of some
category of entities, protocol statements, elementary sensations, basic moral intuitions or what you will as foundations is almost always a feature of some local cognitive
practice, and the denial of the possibility of a ubiquitous
grounding for science and morality is compatible with
universalism, not all local foundational schemes are
objectivist. For example there are different systems of
primary colours, each adequate to a particular task, but
none are grounded in an objective taxonomy of hues. The
grounding moral intuitions of the Judeo-Christian West

are, in the decline of religion, no longer seen even by the staunchest adherents as revelations of objective values.

Antinomies

The term 'antinomy' is used to refer to a situation in which the arguments for and against a pair of polarized positions are inconclusive. One finds reasons in favour of both absolutism and relativism in the interpretation of science, and one also finds reasons for rejecting each opposed position. The upshot of our analyses of the various versions of relativism that have been proposed in our four contexts could be expressed as a series of antinomies. It is our settled opinion that in the debate between relativists and absolutists no other outcome is possible. This result is perhaps unsurprising when we pay attention to the root ideas out of which relativisms and absolutisms are constructed, and the many combinations that are possible, as we have illustrated in the above table. However to refine our intuition we need to focus in a little more sharply on the kinds of oppositions from which the polarities that are at the heart of the relativist antinomies ultimately derive.

Some principles of polar opposition

Using the distinctions between universalism, objectivism and foundationalism, and working with domains of discourse in which there is a use for a concept of truth that is governed by a bivalent grammar, we have been able to set up polar oppositions between various varieties of relativism and absolutism in each of our chosen contexts. Arguments which purported to justify one pole exclusively to the disadvantage of the other were based on a strict dichotomy between truth and falsity. The logical principle shared between many of the arguments we have been using is simple: If the thesis setting out the relativist pole is true then the thesis which expresses the polar opposite must be false. For example if scientific realism, construed as the thesis that every scientific theory is true or false is itself true, then Fleckian relativism is false. Most of the arguments for relativism which purport to oppose what we have called 'frameworks' one against another, are couched in the language of contradiction, a language in which opposition by exclusive dichotomy is the defining principle. An Evil Empire cannot be both morally acceptable (to its citizens) and evil (to us).

Even within the ambience of a bivalent conception of truth the contrast between contradictories that much of our argumentation has assumed is needlessly stark for some of our oppositions. There are other contrasts, for instance there are at least the following: contrariety (two opposing positions cannot be true together but could both be false), incompatibility (if one position seems reasonable the opposing position does not), incongruence (two opposing positions, though both seemingly true and both seemingly making sense cannot be reconciled in one scheme), non-consupponibility (two opposing positions, each itself reasonable, which cannot be supposed or assumed together) and incommensurability (if one has adopted one position the opposing position becomes unintelligible).

In all these cases opposition is not contradiction! While varieties of relativism that would allow contradictory beliefs about the world to be held together must be disallowed, alternative and more modest forms of relativism that allow one to hold pairs of incongruent or incommensurable or incompatible beliefs, each in its appropriate context, may well be allowed. The upshot of our various discussions seems to be that there are irresolvable antinomies, oppositions both poles of which are defensible to some degree. These oppositions, though to describe them we must draw on bipolar truth, need not be the rigidly irreconcilable opposites required by schemes which are modelled on bipolar truth. For the development of this thought we must turn to the writings of Margolis.

Are 'true' and 'false' exclusive and exhaustive assessments of statements?

Throughout the arguments that we have offered for various varieties of relativism and absolutism we have assumed that the sense of such words as 'true' and 'false' was preserved through all the transformations of culture, language, place and time which tempted towards relativism. Only the local criteria changed with context. The very idea of an antinomy depends on the sense of incoherence that attends the seeming demonstration of the truth of opposing positions, doctrines, principles etc. The ubiquitous assumption of bivalence, that there are only truth and falsity and that they exclude each other, has been challenged by Margolis in a number of publications, particularly in his (1991) work *The Truth about Relativism*. We have already encountered Margolis's proposals in discussing existential relativism. At this point we must subject them to critical scrutiny.

To introduce Margolis' insight let us compare the way that the concept of truth and cognate concepts are used in some widely different contexts. In courtrooms the 'grammar' of the concept of 'truth' is fixed by such formulae as 'I swear to tell the *truth*, the whole *truth* and nothing but the *truth*, so help me God'. In the light of the grammatical setting determined by this oath counsel may have recourse to such expressions as a 'pack of lies' to characterize the evidence of a 'hostile' witness. The implication of bivalence is tempting but in courtrooms there is a broad spectrum of alethic concepts at work, from 'reliable', through 'unreliable' to 'lies'. However the implicit recourse to actual states of affairs is also obvious. In evangelical meetings 'witnessing for the truth' is made meaningful by a grammar that is expressed in such formulae as 'the way, the *truth* and the light'. One would be inclined to say that a different concept of 'truth' was used in each context, but in neither the courtroom nor the chapel is the concept 'bivalent'.

In two succinct presentations of his views Margolis (1993a, 1993b) claims that underlying the more superficial relativisms we have been discussing in the preceding chapters, and which we have found to be subject to antinomies, there is a deeper and fully inescapable relativism. We have noted its presence, so to say, at several places. It is now time to lay it out in detail and consider it carefully. If Margolis is right the modest conclusion to which our studies have been tending is at best superficial and at worst mistaken. Margolis's position is based upon 'the need to distinguish questions regarding "the *meaning* of 'true' "' from questions regarding the grounds for making truth-claims – that is, *alethic* and *epistemic* questions' (Margolis, 1993b: 164–5). We take it that this is the familiar distinction drawn by the 'objective idealists' and exemplified in Blanshard's (1939) discussion of truth. This need arises for Margolis (1993a: 2) from the fact that 'interpretations often appear to be incompatible, are reasonably taken to be incompatible, and are construed as *bona fide* truth claims; and yet, in spite of that, we find ourselves disposed to think that incompatible interpretive claims may be conjointly confirmed or validated and the practice may be legitimated'. How can this possibly be? Only if we distinguish alethic relativism, that the meaning of 'true' depends on context and project, from the grounds for making judgements of truth, with whatever meaning. Alethic relativism, it becomes clear, is the idea that there are other assessment values than the 'true' and 'false' that figure in bivalent schemes, for example that which underlies our own attempt to disclose antinomies in each context in which relativist views have been strongly advocated. According to Margolis some of these other values are multivalent, and conform to different grammars from any bivalent scheme.

Some weasel words are in need of careful interpretation here. Margolis' treatment is very cryptic, so we admit we elaborate at our hazard. The first word that needs attention is 'incompatible'. It cannot mean 'contradictory' or 'contrary' since these relations conform to a bivalent grammar. We guess that for Margolis it means 'would be contradictory or contrary if construed according to a bivalent grammar of "true/false" '. With this in hand we can now understand Margolis' main principle that 'Anyone who wishes to construe interpretative judgements as truth-claims or assertions would be well advised . . . to replace (in the sector of the inquiry in question) bivalence [grammar] with a many-valued logic'. (Margolis, 1993a: 3). Cryptically, nay delphically, Margolis then says this 'is the essential alethic motivation for a viable relativism but is not itself a form of relativism' (loc. cit.). Things become clearer below where we are told that 'relativistic logics are a subset of many valued logics that replace bivalent truth-values with other values (call these, also, truth-values or truth-like values), that is alethic

options that do not add a third value "indeterminate" to
the otherwise bivalent pair "true" and "false" '. We take
this to mean that we cannot (should not?) conceive of any
alternative scheme of propositional assessment as a three
valued logic with 'truth' and 'false' as the extreme values.
Margolis's point here may be that this way of resolving
the implausibility of the use of the stark distinction 'true/
false' in all contexts really retains it. If we insert a value
such as 'indeterminate' between 'true' and 'false' we must
mean 'indeterminate as to truth or falsity', and that only
makes sense if 'true' and 'false' are bivalent.

Margolis (1993a) further qualifies his account with
another caveat: 'bivalent and many-valued logics may be
used conjointly provided only their range of applications
are suitably segregated from one another' (loc. cit.).
'Conjointly' is the weasel word here. It cannot mean 'over
the same range of application' that is presumably 'about
the same subject matter' unless that is heavily qualified. It
may mean 'in the same discourse'. Could it be like this: 'It
is bivalently true that Leonardo painted the *Last Supper*,
but considered as a Christian icon it is a failure, whereas
considered as an exemplar of horizontal design it is a great
success.' The judgements 'It is a failure' and 'It is a success'
are incompatible because, if they were assessed bivalently
they would be contradictory. But this cannot be it, since
'failure' and 'success' are contextually segregated, in the
wake of a segregation of the domain of bivalent ('true/
false') logic from multivalent ('success'/'gets by'/'failure')
logic, since it is a success in one context and a failure in
another! This is not a covert revival of bivalence since the
segregated contexts are not mutually exhaustive of critical
domains. In a third domain the proper assessment of the
Last Supper is that it gets by, say as portraiture. The recent
Ring production in Beyreuth has attracted such epithets as

'wonderfully original', 'boring' and 'scandalous betrayal of the Wagnerian heritage'. These differences must not be partitioned by reference to the same kind of domain differentiation as separates the application of bivalent truth from multivalent assessment schemes. Consistent with Margolis' insight explanations of the diversity of judgements of the painting and the production of the opera cycle should focus on diversity of criteria of judgement, not on differences in the multivalence of 'truth-like' concepts. These examples are at best analogues of Margolis's alethic relativism. The segregation of domains is marked by the use of 'truth-like' modes of assessment, in the non-bivalent domain. Perhaps Margolis has in mind concepts like 'correct' and 'incorrect', which naturally expand into a non-bivalent spectrum of assessments. We could ask what is the true value of the velocity of light 'c', in some domain of enquiry, say theoretical physics, and what is the correct value of 'c' in another domain of enquiry, say experimental physics. In the second domain different values for 'c' would not contradict one another.

In all of this alethic and criterial diversity there is a common thread, a thread which must be there for the Margolis analysis to make sense, that is that there is some 'it' which is the common object of consideration in each domain. If the objecthood of the painting disintegrated so that there were to be one art object per domain then we would be looking simply at a loosely linked sequence of independent discourses about different subject matters, and no version of relativism would have been thereby illustrated. It seems that ontological absolutism is a necessary condition for alethic relativism. Margolis plays with the idea of ontological diversity to go along with alethic diversity, for example with respect to what counts as an entity in a domain of artifacts, but this seems both unnecessary and inconsistent with the requirements of alethic relativism in the natural sciences. There is something in nature of which the value of 'c' is a measure.

There is another covert 'absolute' at work in Margolis's scheme. His ingenious account of incompatible judgements in terms of what (counterfactually) would be our assessment of them were they assessed by reference to a bivalent truth scheme imports the concept of bivalence deep into the workings of judgements in the non-bivalent domains, the existence of which is the necessary support for alethic relativism, Margolis style. This strikes us as somewhat similar to the way that postmodernists presuppose the necessary conditions for the possibility of language to hold in every contrasting context, since in each it is diversity of *language* that engenders relativism!

We think it would be correct to say that Margolis holds that demonstrations that there are differences in the criteria for assessing the truth and falsity of propositions is a banal matter, so that to the extent that epistemic relativism is based on such a banality it is of little interest. The same deflation would apply to semantic, ontological and moral relativisms that also depended on variability in criteria of assessment of alethic dichotomies the grammars of which were simply assumed to be transcultural. It is not banal to point out that some domains call for bivalent and others call for multivalent grammars of assessment categories.

The structure of antinomies

In bringing together our arguments we need to acknowledge both first and second order antinomies. At the first order there may be no resolution between those who interpret quantum probabilities as properties of ensembles and those who interpret them as propensities of singular set-ups. At the second order there may be no resolution between those who believe science to be progressive and those who deny this. If there are incommensurable frameworks or conceptual schemes, as Collingwood and Kuhn and others affirm, there could be no neutral overarching standards in virtue of which a rational adjudication between them could be made. Yet the mutual non-translatability of such schemes does not prohibit one from pursuing each in turn – much as a bilingual uses 'one language and then another – all the while constrained by such practical matters as the seemingly obvious requirement that one must speak one language at a time[1] or by the different aims inherent in each framework. Those planning moon-shots do not need to take account of relativity. Frameworks may indeed 'clash' in some ways but clashes need not necessarily take the form of logical contradiction. Many scientific theories are not of universal application yet in a modest way they are objective and even serve to set the foundational conditions for certain projects and certain bodies of practical knowledge, such as how to intercept the trajectory of a comet, and what to do about a cholera epidemic.

From the argument that no method is available that will lead science to the truth (in a propositional sense of correspondence), it does not follow that we have no rational way of improving upon our science or that we have made no progress. To assume that progress can be understood exclusively in terms of increments in truths in the correspondence sense and the elimination of falsehoods begs the question. Coherentists may, with different terms of reference, speak as convincingly about progress in science as the correspondentist may. Progress does not drop out of the coherentist's account; it is construed differently. The point is that it is a mistake to assume that without truth in a correspondence sense there is no way to choose objectively among competing cognitive commitments independently of human thought and practice. We have demonstrated this with the most subtle of all philosophies of physics, the neo-Kantian 'affordance' theory of Niels Bohr. In a sense Bohrian phenomena are not objective, since there is an ineliminable component provided by the humanly contrived apparatus. Nor are Bohrian phenomena universal, since with different apparatus the world affords something different. But they are foundational for the science of high energy and particle physics, a typical case of *local* foundationalism.

One might argue that relativism requires that claims in different frames or schemes must compete, if not in the strong sense of contradicting one another, then at least in some such weaker sense such as being incongruent. For two claims to disagree they must disagree about something which is held common. Without such commonality the claims would talk about different things; they would be passing each other by. If, for example, the lexicon of Aristotelian physics really is untranslatable into Newtonian physics (or vice versa), and if on that account they talk about 'different worlds' as Kuhn suggests, then the question of relativism does not even arise, since strictly speaking they would not be talking about the same thing. In order for there to be genuine conflict, however one construes the logical terms of that conflict, there must be commonality of the objects to which they presumably refer. As well, there must be sufficient commonality in the concepts deployed in their descriptions. Without such commonality genuine cases of conflict cannot be formulated, nor can genuine examples of relativist resolutions of such conflicts be found. So the concession that there might be genuine cases of incommensurability is not tantamount to a concession of the strongest possible form of relativism. For instance Margolis (1989) allows for a commonality of the object of interpretation, where there is commensuration of referring expressions, but where competing claims about the common object are opposed in some opposition that is logically weaker than contradiction, he proposes a supervenient ontological multiplicity: 'when one realises that the canvas is by van Meegerhen, it's the same paint as before but a different art object'. We believe that we are correct in interpreting Margolis as holding that there is a flux both in culture and in nature. In the end, for him, the relation between nature and science is to be construed as a species of the relation between art objects and art discourses, such as criticism and history. Both the objects addressed and the concepts and grammars of the discourses addressing them are in flux. The case for the flux in the context of art objects is surely unassailable. What we take a natural object to be is, in real science, an aspect of that object, a discovery of a capacity in nature that is realized in some experimental set-up, and would not be revealed in the manner that it is in any other set-up. The parallel between art discourse and science discourse is a very limited one.

It has often been pointed out that there are no descriptions of objects, phenomena, states of affairs and so on that are wholly independent of historically constituted practices and the institutions in which they are made intelligible and plausible. One might concede the point to such an intentionalism (or some would say historicism) without admitting any strong relativism. It is possible to hold, as a coherentist might, that there are no concepts or terms intelligible independently of their place in some framework or scheme, but that in the long run one ought to embrace only those claims that are coherently related to other claims in the pertinent framework. In other words, a coherentist might well believe that all conflicting claims would gradually be reconciled in an ever emerging and enlarging scheme or framework. Such a position accommodates an intentionalism or historicism *and* resists some varieties of relativism. However, and here we meet a second order antinomy, a relativist might well respond with the observation that nothing in this argument eliminates the possibility that there may be two or more ever-enlarging schemes, all adequate to the phenomena.

Paradoxes

The argument that relativism is self-refuting is well-worn, and we have examined versions of the argument in the appropriate contexts. If relativism is true there are no propositions that are true in all contexts. But that proposition must be true in all contexts. There is then a proposition that is absolute in the sense that it expresses a universal truth. If there is a universal truth relativism is false. So if it is true relativism is false. But before we abandon ourselves to paradox consider Collingwood's suggestions that constellations of absolute presuppositions are neither true nor false. They are merely supposed, and necessarily so given the sorts of cultural beings that we happen to be. The question of rational justification *at this level* does not arise. Now, there is nothing contradictory about saying that at this level reasons which would demonstrate truth (or falsity) of absolute presuppositions must give out. How we do come to hold such propositions is neither here nor there.

Collingwood's scheme suggests two possible ways of construing the generic thesis of relativism itself, instantiated in any of the contexts we have examined. As a relative presupposition it could be either truth or false. So as a relative presupposition relativism could be affirmed as true, but not as absolutely true, since nothing in the scheme is absolutely true. And the paradox is by-passed. Alternatively, taken as an absolute presupposition, relativism would be neither truth nor false. In such a case the very possibility of the charge of self refutation does not arise. That charge would stick only if it is the case that what is affirmed as relatively true is also affirmed as absolutely true. But that is just what the Collingwoodian proposal rules out.

A similar line of argument can be found in the writings of Wittgenstein (1953). There is an important class of propositions that express the boundaries of meaningful discourses. Such propositions are always true, but their negations are not false. They are meaningless. If the proposition that something cannot be both red and green all over at once expresses a rule for the meaningful use of the words 'red' and 'green' then the proposition 'Something can be red and green all over at once' is not false but meaningless. Framework propositions are 'grammatical', in Wittgenstein's broad use of that expression. Relativism and the various absolutisms that stand in opposition are expressed in framework propositions which delineate the boundary between sense and nonsense. The paradoxes of relativism depend on the opposition between truth and falsity for both a statement and its negation, and that presupposes that both are meaningful. It is to just these cases that Wittgenstein's insight applies. There cannot be self-refuting paradoxes for framework propositions.

Our Position

In brief summary where have we arrived at the end of this discussion? We hold that there are no concepts which are applicable at all times and in all circumstances and in all linguistic communities. There is no store of ultimately illuminating concepts which, if correctly predicated of a clearly identified array of stable objects would produce the eternal truths after which all dedicated persons of ideas strive. Concepts are social products and are applicable in so far as thinkers of a common tradition find them useful. There is no common standard of utility.

We are never cognitively nor semantically 'prior to' communities. We find ourselves *in* them, in virtue of our development as appropriators of the common procedures of our culture, of which our ability to use language and to manipulate symbol systems are the most salient. We do not start in the beginning; we start in the middle.

Assertions and claims about what is and is not real arise from the epistemically prior realization of the coherence of discourse and practice in widely diverse contexts. Such realizations can strike us only in the complex realm of the intimate intertwining of the natural and the artifactual that we have exemplified in the idea of the affordances of experimental apparatus in intimate liaison with the material world. It cannot be based on some privileged access to the way the world is, independent of practice. Non-foundational historicism clearly does not necessitate relativism; nor does it necessitate irrationalism. Most important, in its narrativist form, it promises a way of making sense of the fact that we do, justifiably, reach some consensus about cognitive acceptability. And that is explicable without reifying its procedures into objectivist-foundationalist structures.

In the course of his intellectual development Popper shifted from a foundationalist fallibilism, in which singular basic statements served to definitively falsify mistaken conjectures to a kind of non-foundationalism, in which even the seemingly logically tight claim that a conjecture had been falsified could be asserted only tentatively and provisionally. However, in order to reconcile his emphasis on the rejection of false conjectures with the idea of the progress of science (towards the ever distant goal of truth) he tried to couple an absolutist theory of truth as correspondence with the non-foundational epistemology of his later philosophy. It is instructive that Popper succeeded neither in characterizing the direction of progress from a defective theory to a better one, nor in explaining satisfactorily what the terminus of scientific progress in Truth would be like. One may, perhaps on the strength of the non-foundationalist epistemology, be prompted to drop all talk of absolute truth. Such a strategy might be pressed for reasons given by Schmitt (personal communication) who says 'Since absolute truth is an extrinsic relational feature of systems of beliefs, it follows, given the restriction to intrinsic features, that the notion of absolute truth can play no role in an account of relative revision.' The self-correcting procedures of the disciplines do allow us to distinguish between that which is worthy of belief and that which is not. But perhaps we have now acquired enough wisdom to be content with a modest account of knowledge, rooted in the idea of adequate procedures, and finally abandon the chimera of the correspondence theory of truth, in so far as it based on the idea of an all or none comparison between statements and states of affairs.

Different aspects of the world are available to different kinds of creatures, in so far as their sensory systems differ, and to different groups of human beings in so far as they are differently placed and differently equipped. In this sense knowledge of the world tends to the relative. But all such aspects are aspects of one and the same world, and in that sense knowledge of the world tends to the absolute.

NOTES

1   Creoles and pidgins are linguistic forms that come into being just in so far as people do speak two languages at once!

References

Aquinas, St Thomas *c*.1270 A. C. Pegis (ed.) 1945: *Basic Writings of Saint Thomas Aquinas.* New York: Random House.

Aristotle, 1921: *Politics* trans. B. Jowett, in *The Works of Aristotle* Oxford: The Clarendon Press Vol. X.

Aristotle, 1925: *Nichomachean Ethics* In W. D. Ross, (trans.) *The Works of Aristotle* Oxford: Oxford University Press, Volume IX.

Aronson J., Harré, R. and Way, E. C. 1994: *Realism Rescued* London: Duckworth.

Austin, J. L. 1962: *How to do Things with Words.* Oxford: Clarendon Press.

Austin, J. L. 1979: A plea for excuses In J. O. Urmson and G. J. Warnock (eds), *Philosophical Papers* Oxford University Press.

Bachnick, J. 1982: Deixis and self/other reference in Japanese discourse. In *Sociolinguistic Working Paper* no. 99, Austin (Texas): Southwest Educational Development Library.

Barnes, B. 1977: *Interests and the Growth of Knowledge.* London: Routledge and Kegan Paul.

Becker, A. L. and Oka, G. N. 1974: Person in Kawi: Explorations of an elementary semantic dimension *Oceanic Linguistics* 13.2 and 2, 229–55.

Benedict, R. 1934: *Patterns of Culture.* Boston and New York: Houghton Mifflin.

Bhaskar, R. 1975: *A Realist Theory of Science* Leeds: Books.

Blanshard, B. 1939: *The Nature of Thought* chaps XXV and XXXVI. London: George Allen and Unwin.

Bloor, D. 1976: *Knowledge and Social Imagery*. London: Routledge and Kegan Paul.

Boas, F. 1928: *Anthropology and Modern Life* New York: Norton.

Bohr, N. 1963: *Essays (1958–64) of Atomic Physics and Human Knowledge*. New York: Wiley.

Brink, D. O. 1989: *Moral Realism and the Foundations of Ethics*. Cambridge: Cambridge University Press.

Collingwood, R. G. 1940: *Essay on Metaphysics*. Oxford: Clarendon Press.

Conway, G. D. 1989: *Wittgenstein on Foundations*. Atlantic Highlands, N.J.: Humanities Press.

Davidson, D. 1984: *Inquiries into Truth and Interpretation*. Oxford: Clarendon Press.

Davies, B. and Harré, R. 1990: Positioning. *Journal for the Theory of Social Behaviour*, **20** 43–63.

Evans, G. 1982: *The Varieties of Reference*. Oxford: Clarendon Press.

Feyerabend, P. K. 1975: *Against Method*. London: New Left Books.

Field, H. 1982: Realism and relativism. *Journal of Philosophy* **LXXIX** 553–67.

Finnis, J. 1980: *Natural Law and Natural Rights*. Oxford: Clarendon Press.

Fleck, L. 1921: *Genesis and Development of a Scientific Fact* (trans. F. Bradley and T. J. Trenn 1979). Chicago: University of Chicago Press.

Frege, G. 1952: On source and meaning. In P. Geach and M. Black (eds) *Philosophical Writings of G. Frege*. Oxford: Blackwell.

Fuller, L. 1978: *The Morality of Law*. New Haven: Yale University Press.

Geertz, C. 1973: *The Interpretation of Cultures* New York: Basic Books.

Gergen, K. J. 1991: *The Saturated Self.* New York: Basic Books.

Gibson, J. J. 1966: *The Senses Considered as Perceptual Systems.* Boston: Houghton Mifflin.

Goffman, E. 1963: *Stigma.* Englewood Cliffs, N.J.: Prentice Hall.

Goodman, N. 1978: *Ways of World Making.* Indianapolis: Hackett.

Goodman, N. 1982: Language and ontology. In W. Leinfellner, L. E. Kraemer and J. Schank (eds), *Proceedings of the 6th International Wittgenstein Symposium,* Vienna.

Gray, J. 1994: *Isaiah Berlin.* London: Harper Collins.

Griffin, J. 1986: *Well-being.* Oxford: Clarendon Press.

Harman, G. 1977: *The Nature of Morality.* New York: Oxford University Press.

Harré, R. 1963: *Matter and Method.* London: Macmillan.

Harré, R. 1983: *Personal Being.* Oxford: Blackwell.

Harré, R. 1986: *Varieties of Realism.* Oxford: Blackwell.

Harré, R. and Gillett, G. 1994: *The Discursive Mind.* London and Los Angeles: Sage.

Harris, M. 1974: *Cows, Pigs, Wars and Witches.* New York: Random House.

Harris, R. 1981: *The Language Makers.* Oxford: Pergamon.

Harrison, B. 1985: Kant and the sincere fanatic In S. C. Brown (ed.), *Philosophers of the Eighteenth Century*: London.

Hart, H. L. A. 1975: *The Concept of Law.* Oxford: Clarendon Press.

Hatch, E. 1983: *Culture and Morality: the relativity of values in anthropology.* New York: Columbia University Press.

Hesse, M. B. 1980: *Revolutions and Reconstructions in the Philosophy of Science.* Bloomington, Indiana: Indiana University Press.

Hill, A. O. 1986: *Mother Tongue: Father Time.* Bloomington, Indiana: Indiana University Press.

Holiday, A. 1988: *Moral Powers.* Brighton: Harvester.

Hollway, W. 1984: Gender differences and the production of subjectivity. In J. Henriques et al, *Changing the Subject,* London: Methuen.

Hookway, C. 1988: *Quine: Language, Experience and Reality.* Cambridge: Polity Press.

Hume, D. 1740 [1978] *A Treatise of Human Nature* ed. L. A. Selby-Bigge, Oxford: The Clarendon Press.

Hume, D. 1748 [1951] *An Enquiry Concerning the Human Understanding* ed. L. A. Selby-Bigge, Oxford: The Clarendon Press.

Jakobson, R. 1957: *Shifters, Verbal Categories and the Russian Verb* Cambridge: Russian Language Department.

Kant, I. 1781 trans. N. Kemp Smith 1934 [1781]: *Critique of Pure Reason.* Konigsberg, London: Macmillan.

Kant, I. [1781] *Groundwork of the Metaphysics of Morals* [trans. H. J. Paton, New York: Harper and Row 1964].

Katz, J. J. 1977: *Propositional Structure and Illocutionary Acts.* New York: Crowell.

Kenny, A. 1992: *Aristotle on the Perfect Life.* Oxford: Clarendon Press.

Krausz, M. 1991: Crossing cultures: two universalisms and two relativisms. In M. Dascal (ed.), *Cultural Relativism and Philosophy*, Leiden and New York: E. J. Brill.

Krausz, M. 1993: *Rightness and Reason: interpretation in cultural practices.* Ithaca, N.Y.: Cornell University Press.

Kuhn, T. S. 1970: *The Structure of Scientific Revolutions.* Chicago: University of Chicago Press.

Lackoff, G. 1981: *Women, Fire and Dangerous Things.* Chicago: Chicago University Press.

Laudan, L. 1981: The pseudo-science of science? *Philosophy of Social Science*, **11** 179.

Lee, D. 1950: Notes on the comparison of self amongst the Wintu. In *Journal of Abnormal and Social Psychology*, **45** 538–43.

Lloyd, Lord 1985: *Introduction to Jurisprudence.* London: Stevens and Sons, ch. 3.

Lutz, C. 1988: *Unnatural Emotions.* Chicago and London: Chicago University Press.

MacIntyre, A. 1977: Epistemological crises, dramatic narrative and the philosophy of science. *The Monist*, **60** 468–69.

MacIntyre, A. 1989: Relativism, power and philosophy. In M. Krausz (ed.) *Relativism: interpretation and Confrontation*. Notre Dame: Notre Dame University Press.

Mandelbaum, M. 1982: Subjective, objective and conceptual relativism. In J. W. Meiland and M. Krausz (eds), *Relativism: cognitive and moral*. Notre Dame: Notre Dame University Press.

Manicas, R. P. and Rosenberg, A. 1985: Naturalism, epistemological individualism and the 'Strong Programme' in the sociology of knowledge. *Journal for the Theory of Social Behaviour, 15* 76–101.

Manicas, R. P. and Rosenberg, A. 1988: The sociology of scientific knowledge: can we ever get it straight? *Journal for the Theory of Social Behaviour, 18* 51–76.

Margolis, J. 1980: *Art and Philosophy*. Atlantic Highlands, N.J.: Humanities Press.

Margolis, J. 1989: The novelty of Marx's theory of practice, *Journal for the Theory of Social Behaviour, 19* 367–88.

Margolis, J. 1991: *The Truth about Relativism*. Oxford: Blackwell.

Margolis, J. 1993a: *The Flux of History and the Flux of Science*. Chicago: Chicago University Press.

Margolis, J. 1993b: Reply to Sonja Kreidl-Rinofner. *Graz Philosophische Studien*, 163–186.

Margolis, J. 1994: Plain talk about interpretation on a relativistic model. *Journal of Aesthetics and Art Criticism*, 1–7.

Mauntner, F. 1901: *Contributions to a Critique of Language*. Vienna.

Mink, L. O. 1978: Narrative form as a cognitive instrument. In R. H. Canary and H. Kozicki (eds) *The Writing of History: literary form and historical understanding*. Madison, Wisconsin: University of Wisconsin Press.

Much, N. C. 1995: Becoming the mother. In R. Harré and P. Stearns (eds), *Rethinking*. London and Los Angeles: Sage, Volume III.

Muhlhausler, P. and Harré, R. 1991: *Pronouns and People*. Oxford: Blackwell.

Nowell-Smith, P. N. S. 1954: *Ethics*. London: Penguin.

Papineau, D. 1979: *Theory and Meaning*. Oxford: Clarendon Press, Chap. 5.

Peirce, C. S. 1940: *The Philosophy of Peirce* ed. L. Buchler London: Routledge and Kegan Paul.

Plato 1953: *Theaetetus* trans. B. Jowett, *The Dialogues of Plato*. Oxford: Clarendon Press, Volume III.

Popper, K. R. 1972: *Objective Knowledge*. Oxford: Clarendon Press.

Quine, W. V. 1952: *From a Logical Point of View*. Cambridge, Mass.: Harvard University Press.

Quine, W. V. 1969: *Ontological Relativity and Other Essays*. New York: Columbia University Press.

Quine, W. V. 1975: On empirically equivalent systems of the world. *Erkenntnis*, **9** 313–28.

Radcliffe-Brown, A. R. 1952: *Structure and Function in Primitive Society*. London: Cohen and West.

Rorty, R. 1980: *Philosophy and the Mirror of Nature*. Oxford: Blackwell.

Rorty, R. 1989: *Contingency, Irony and Solidarity*. Cambridge: Cambridge University Press.

Sabat, S. and Harré, R. 1992: The construction and deconstruction of self in Alzheimer's disease. *Ageing and Society*, **12** 443–61.

Sahlins, M. 1978: Culture as protein and profit. *New York Review of Books*, xxv 23 Nov. 45–53.

Schmitt, F. 'Relative truth and relative revision' Personal communication.

Searle, J. R. 1979: *Expression and Meaning*. Cambridge: Cambridge University Press.

Shotter, J. and Gergen, K. J. 1987: *Texts of Identity*. London: Sage.

Siegel, H. 1987: *Relativism Refuted: a critique of contemporary epistemological relativism*. Dordrecht: Reidel.

Toulmin, S. E. 1961: *Foresight and Understanding*. London: Hutchinson.

Urban, G. 1987: The 'I' of discourse. In Lee, B. and Urban, G. (eds), *Semiotics, Self and Society*, Mouton de Gruyter. Berlin and New York, pp. 27–52.

van Fraassen, B. 1980: *The Scientific Image*. Oxford: Clarendon Press.

Waismann, F. 1968: *How I see Philosophy*. London: Macmillan.

Wertsch, J. 1985: *Vygotsky and the Social Formation of Mind*. Cambridge, Mass.: Harvard University Press.

Whewell, W. 1847 [1945]: *The Philosophy of the Inductive Sciences*. London: Parker.

Whorf, B. L. 1956: *Language, Thought and Reality*. Cambridge, Mass.: MIT Press.

Wierzbicka, A. 1992: *Semantics, Cognition and Culture*. New York and Oxford: Oxford University Press.

Wittgenstein, L. 1953: *Philosophical Investigations*. Oxford: Blackwell.

Wittgenstein, L. 1969: *On Certainty*. Oxford: Blackwell.

Wittgenstein, L. 1992: *Tractatus Logico-Philosophicus*. London.

Name Index

Aquinas, St T. 175–8, 183
Aristotle 17, 18, 122, 124, 171
Aston, F. 82
Austin, J. L. 158

Barnes, B. 99, 102, 103, 107
Bellarmine, Cardinal 112
Benedict, R. 156
Berlin, I. 30, 183, 186
Bhaskar, R. 120
Blanshard, B. 184
Bloor, D. 99, 103, 106, 107
Boas, G. 156
Bohr, N. 130–4, 138, 218
Brink, D. O. 166, 183, 184

Collingwood, R. G. 76, 84–9, 94

Davidson, D. 36, 95
Davy, H. 62
Descartes, R. 141

Evans, G. 57, 58

Feyerabend, P. 78, 190–5, 206
Field, H. 29

Finnis, J. 174, 178–82, 183
Fleck, L. 75
Frege, G. 60

Galileo, G. 112, 122, 193
Gergen, K. J. 190, 196–9, 206
Gibson, J. J. 132
Goffman, E. 48, 162
Goodman, N. 27, 79, 113–17, 120, 125
Goodstein, R. L. 122, 123
Griffin, J. 167, 168

Harman, G. 161, 163
Harris, M. 159, 160
Harrison, B. 59, 186, 187, 188
Hart, H. L. A. 174, 175
Hatch, E. 157
Hesse, M. 106, 107
Holiday, A. 31, 32, 198

Jacobson, R. 44

Kant, I. 16, 18, 19, 20, 31, 150, 151, 154
Kuhn, T. S. 9, 75–80, 83, 84

Laudan, L. 106

Lavoisier, A. 78
Lee, D. 47
Lloyd, Lord 173
Lutz, C. 12, 65

McIntyre, A. 90, 96
Mandelbaum, M. 96
Manicus, P. 100, 101
Margolis, J. 7, 33, 98, 138,
    142–7, 211–16
Mill, J. S. 83, 122
Mink, L. O. 91, 92
Much, N. 65

Nowell-Smith, P. 168

Pasteur, H. 122
Peirce, C. S. 143
Plato 36, 72
Popper, K. R. 70, 192, 223
Priestley, J. 78
Protagoras 72, 74

Quine, W. V. 9, 28, 36, 53–9,
    61, 64

Radcliffe-Brown, A. R. 158,
    159, 160
Rorty, R. 190, 199–206
Rosenberg, A. 100, 101
Russell, B. 34

Sahlins, M. 150
St Augustine 34
Siegel, H. 29, 96, 136

Toulmin, S. E. 77

Waismann, F. 61, 62
Whewell, W. 9, 14, 76
Whorf, B. L. 194
Wierzbicka, A. 41, 42, 46, 50,
    51, 52, 64
Wittgenstein, L. 20, 21, 32, 37,
    39, 52, 62, 107, 221

Subject Index

absolute presuppositions 84–9
  assessment as relativist 88–91
  meaning relations 86
  question–answer hierarchies
    86–7
  relative presuppositions 85
absolutisms, varieties 207
affordances 132, 134–5
anthropological insight
    (Aristotle) 14, 16–18
antinomies 209–20
  polar oppositions in 209–11
  structure of 216–20
  truth and alternative
    assessments 211–16
antirelativist arguments 26–32
  paradoxes 26–30
  transcendental arguments 30–2
aptness discriminations 146–7
artifacts
  existence of 141–2
  identity of 142–6

bivalence and many-valued
    logics 214–15
Bohr's philosophy of science
    130–5
  complementarity principle 132

correspondence principle 132

capping of relativisms 15, 17,
  20, 21
categorical imperative (Kantian)
  150–2
  universalist assumptions in
    151–2
classification and language 121–2
constructionist insight (Kant) 14,
  18–20
culture
  concept of 11–14
  'psychological' element 12
  'science' element 13
  'social' element 14

dispositions, as real properties
  108

epistemic frameworks 75–94
epistemic relativism 68–110
  global arguments against 94–6
  paradoxes of 96–9
  and semantic relativism
    109–10
'erosion of the self' 196
essences, denial of 203–4
'exists' and 'exists for' 122–4

fabricating v. finding 116
fallacy, epistemological 120–1
   family resemblance 191, 200–1
Finnis's radical individualism
   178–82
   desiderata for human
   flourishing 181–2
Fleckian relativism 112–13
forms of life, human and tribal
   66–7

incommensurability 9, 79–82
   and cosmologies 194–5
indexicality of moralities 160–1
indexical manifolds 45–6
individualism in epistemology
   109

knowledge as justified true belief
   68

language and moral universals
   199
languages as tools 34–6

meaning, absolutist accounts
   language comparisons 47–8
   object signified, arguments
      against 38–41
   object signified, arguments for
      37–8
   universal root vocabulary,
      arguments against 42–52
meaning and context 55–64
   family resemblance 63–4
   Lutz on emotions 65
   Much on 'possession' 65
   'open texture of language' 61

'systematicity of language'
   62–3
methodological fallibilism,
   weaknesses 71
moral absolutisms 165–85
moral assessment, alternative
   systems 164–5
moral facts 166
   diversity of 169–70
   as preferences 168–9
moralities of honour 161–4
moralities and maxims 150–1
moral realism and natural
   science 166–7
moral relativism 149–88
   anthropological arguments for
      156–60
   and coherence of life 183–5
   forms of 155
   philosophical arguments for
      160–5
   universalist assumptions in
      152–4
moral systems, doubts about
   186–8
moving boundary argument 121

natural law as absolutist
   morality 173–83
   a posteriori and a priori
      arguments 173–4
   divine law and natural law
      176, 177
   eternal law and natural law
      176, 177, 178
   natural law and moral
      teleology 175–8
   natural law and prudential
      teleology 174–5

natural science
  v. artistic activity 200
  v. psychological studies 203–4
needs as a basis for morality 170

ontological relativism 116–48
  epistemological groundings 135–7
  paradox of 137–41
  realism 138–9
  specification of 113

paradigms 77–9
  change of 77–9
  comparison of 78
  normal science 77
  rational choice among 79
  standards of evaluation of 83–4
  world-defining 82–3
paradox of relativist self-refutation 220–1
  Collingwood's escpae route 221
  Wittgenstein's framework propositions 221
personal responsibility abrogated 198
persons and relativism 154–5
persons and their beliefs 68–9
Popper's World Three 70–1
positioning 48–9
pronouns and indexical expressions 42–52
  Japanese 50
  Kawi 48
  Wintu 47
propositional truth rejected 201

propositions and the world 202–3
Protagorean relativism 72–4, 97, 112

qualitative and numerical identity confused 197

radical translation 9, 53–9
  as Machian reduction 56
  Quine's arguments 54–5
realism in contemporary philosophy of science 205–6
  laws as prescriptions for model building 205
  models as correspondents with the world 205–6
relativism
  catalogued by negation 24
  catalogued by topic 23–4
  discursive, arguments for 7–9
  evaluative, degrees of 74–5
  Fleckian 75–84
  ontological 9–11
  permissive (benign) 3–4
  roots of 2
  sceptical (malign) 3–4
  strong and weak 25
  varieties 23–5; foundationalist 5, 6; objectivist 5, 6; universalist 4, 6

semantic insight (Wittgenstein) 14, 20–2
semantic relativism 34–7
  arguments for 53–66
'slide into anarchy' 191
solipsism 10

Strong Programme 99–109
  and cognitive psychology of
    perception 107–8
  four main tenets, causality,
    impartiality, reflexivity,
    symmetry 101
  objections to causality
    principle 104–5
  objections to impartiality
    principle 105–6
  objections to reflexivity
    principle 106–7
  objections to symmetry
    principle 106
  realist aspects 102–7
strong relativisms 190
  and scientific method 192–6

taxonomic priority thesis 57
theory-fact relations 76
thought-collective and thought-
  style
tolerance, principle of 158–9
traditions, distinctive 89–91

historical 'facts' within 91–3,
  94
narrative intelligibility 90–1,
  93
translation manuals v. theories
  of meaning 57–9
truth 7
  assumption of 32
  correspondence and coherence
    126

umwelt 128–9
unicity and individuality 142–6

version relativity 128
versions, world 113, 114, 115–17
version-sensitivity of categories
  117–20
virtue and personhood 171–2

well-being 170–1
world,
  criteriological role 125–6
  regulative role 125–6, 128–9